THE LINE

Public Art in East London

THE LINE

The Line is East London's public art trail. Its route follows the waterways and the line of the Greenwich Meridian, offering a journey through a dynamic urban landscape where everyone can explore art, nature and heritage for free. It opened to the public in 2015.

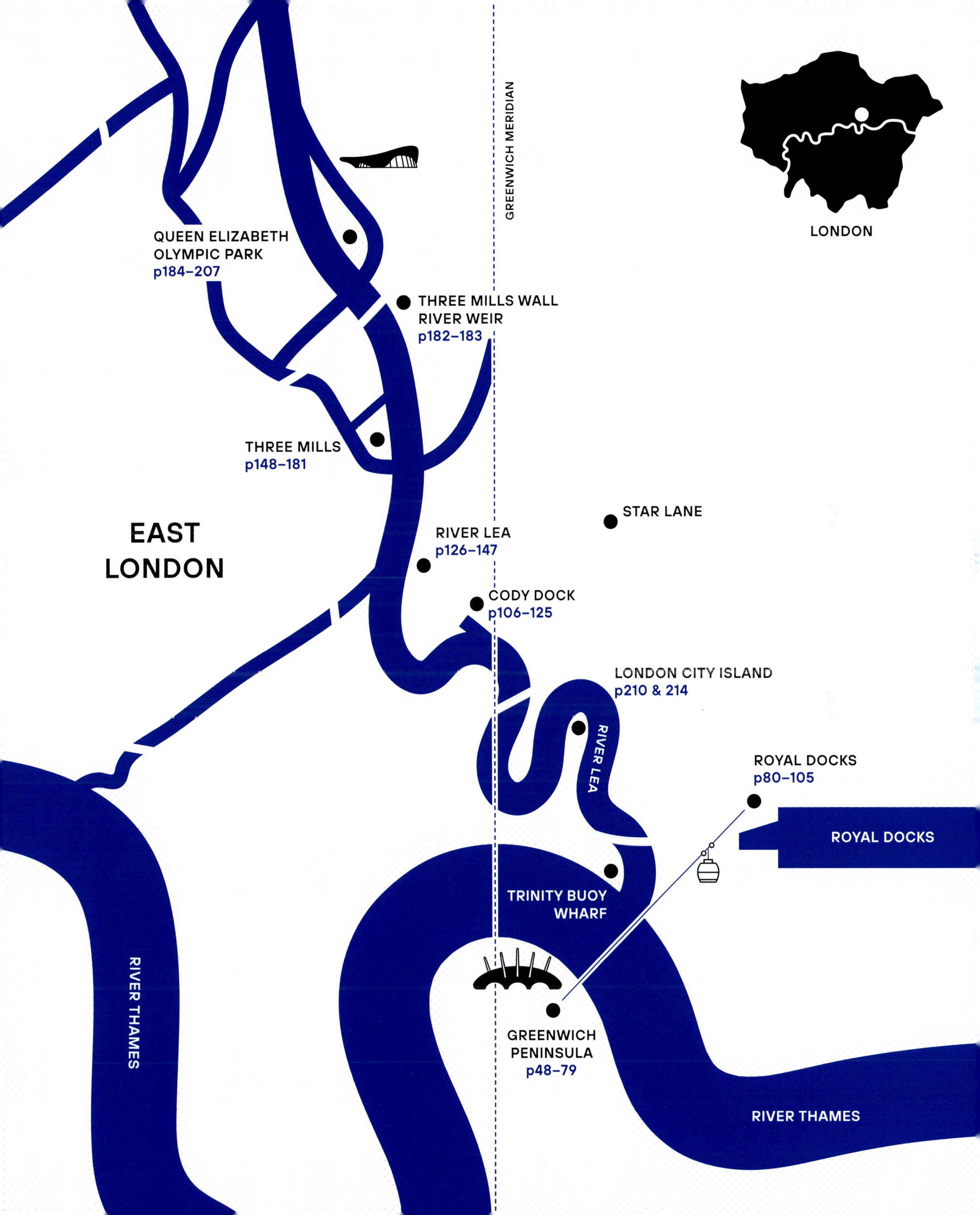
LONDON
GREENWICH MERIDIAN
QUEEN ELIZABETH
OLYMPIC PARK
p184–207
THREE MILLS WALL
RIVER WEIR
p182–183
THREE MILLS
p148–181
EAST
LONDON
STAR LANE
RIVER LEA
p126–147
CODY DOCK
p106–125
LONDON CITY ISLAND
p210 & 214
RIVER LEA
ROYAL DOCKS
p80–105
ROYAL DOCKS
TRINITY BUOY
WHARF
RIVER THAMES
GREENWICH
PENINSULA
p48–79
RIVER THAMES

FOREWORD
SARAH CARRINGTON

'Traveler, your footprints
are the only road, nothing else.
Traveler, there is no road;
you make your own path as you walk.'

Antonio Marchado

The origin of the word *learn* is 'to follow' or to 'find a track'.[1] For the last ten years, The Line has forged a path along East London's historic waterways, learning about people and places – as well as developing new approaches to working in the public realm – along the way. Thanks to the combined charm, tenacity and inventiveness of its founders, the simple idea of bringing works of art that were previously hidden inside, outdoors – and making art accessible to all – came to life and has endured. The Line is at once an experience, a place, and a connected web of people, relationships and memory.

This book marks an important milestone, one which at times felt like it would never come about. Public art should appear seamless, magically emerging in the landscape. The reality of installing works of art (over 40 since 2015) along a route that crosses three boroughs and has involved approximately twenty landowners is far from straightforward. The process can take many months (often years) of planning, layers of investment, delicate negotiation and complex agreements. Installations may require explorations of underground services, surveys of the flight paths of birds, bat behaviours or tide levels. Fundamentally, it is a process that relies on an open spirit and collaboration.

The Line's staying power is a testament to the determined efforts of the late Clive Dutton OBE and Megan Piper to win hearts and minds back in 2015, and then to Megan for her grace and persistence, putting one foot in front of the other to continue to make the vision a reality. It has also benefitted from an extraordinary bedrock of goodwill and support. Without the many artists, galleries, landowners, stakeholders, community partners and supporters who have come on the journey, the project would have remained just an idea.

The path of The Line follows the waterways through East London, where sculptures mark the route and draw local residents and visitors into this charged urban landscape. A number of the works on The Line explore the politics of water in the city, and how these flows have shaped and defined London's growth and global connections along the line of the Greenwich Meridian (the project's namesake) and beyond. Larry Achiampong's work *Sanko-time*, commissioned by The Line in 2020, weaves together archival sound with local school children chanting their self-penned mantra 'we are one, we are the same'. The work, developed during COVID lockdowns and against the backdrop of Black Lives Matter protests around the world, included voices from the Windrush generation and revealed the lasting legacies of the Royal Docks and River Thames as key points in empire building. Further north, Helen Cammock's work, *On WindTides*, co-commissioned by The Line with local residents and supported by Newham Council, was launched in 2024. It reflects on the River Lea – its tides and the movement of communities drawn by the industries along the water's edge.

The Line was first formed as a join-the-dots of sorts, linking together different areas through the installation of a series of monumental sculptures along towpaths. This route now creates a cultural backbone for East London, marking a journey for exploration. Over ten years, the project has evolved and proliferated to encompass a breadth of programmes and curatorial approaches, including site-specific sound, film, light, and performance, as the essays and images here show. Artists have revealed and threaded together layers of history, local people have shared stories through collaboration and engagement, performers have danced and floated, and audiences have seen the city anew.

Prior to working at The Line, I worked in Australia for two years, where First Nations cultures describe ancestral routes as 'songlines' – lines which in their becoming represent a process of storytelling and mapping across the landscape. Functioning as repositories of knowledge, the lines connect neighbouring groups, enabling individuals to travel vast distances while marking out features of the landscape. The Line has connected with people and places through navigating a path and in the learning and telling of stories along the way; the route has evolved to form a storehouse of memory.

Like shifting sands and tributaries, The Line has pursued new paths, harnessing the power of the unexpected. Changing installations and artists' responses offer an exhilarating sense of discovery and adventure – instilling the desire to return in different seasons, at different times of day and at different tides, to affirm that what you saw the first time was really there. This publication will take you on a journey, evoking how the installations on the route inhabit and animate the landscape, architecture and structures they occupy, while capturing the atmosphere and experience of the route itself. The Line celebrates the power of public art. The project has traced a path for the last ten years, now imprinted for the future. It has created a space to share stories, weave magic and wonder, open eyes, ask questions and build memories. Having taken the baton from Megan in this tenth anniversary year, I will keep putting one foot in front of the other to build on these well-trodden desire lines and steer the project into its next decade.

Sarah Carrington
Director, The Line

1 Antonio Marchado's poem and the reference to the etymology of *learn* are both referenced in Anita Sethi's book *I Belong Here: A Journey Along the Backbone of Britain*, Bloomsbury Wildlife, 2021.

IN CONVERSATION

MEGAN PIPER AND
GUS CASELY-HAYFORD

Gus Casely-Hayford

Many happy returns. Ten years, how does that feel?

Megan Piper

For the last ten years, I feel we've been running at a pace that means there hasn't been much time for reflection. Particularly over the last five years, the organisation – and the scope and scale of what we've been doing – has expanded significantly. So it's a nice moment for reflection.

GCH And to reflect both to look back, but also to look forward, which is quite exciting. Could we look back just for a little bit because it'd be wonderful to get a sense of the story of The Line, how it came into being with Clive Dutton and that partnership. Can you give me a sense of how you got together and how you came up with this amazing idea for The Line?

MP Clive and I met in 2012. We were introduced through David Bailey, the photographer, who had an exhibition in the Royal Docks.

GCH Because he's a Newham boy, isn't he?

MP He is, and if it weren't for his private view, I may never have met Clive and The Line would almost certainly never have happened ... At the time, Clive was Executive Director of Regeneration and Inward Investment at Newham, which was the main host borough for the Olympic and Paralympic Games. He was one of those people that you meet who had this extraordinary energy. In life, we swap business cards with so many people, but I remember thinking that he was someone I would keep in touch with. Back then, I used to have a gallery in the West End and he would come to private views and we became friends. One day, I said to him I was interested in what he was doing in Newham and what the legacy of the Olympics would really be. By this point, we're probably well into 2013, and he invited me to the council's offices in the Royal Docks and gave the most extraordinary presentation, essentially positioning Newham as the future.

GCH Newham has changed profoundly over the course of the last couple of decades. First, there was the transition to the Olympics, and then, I imagine that the Olympics itself must have had an impact. So, you're talking about that year after the Olympics, so what was it like?

MP Clive talked about the energy that there was in the lead up to – and during – the Olympics and the investment in the area, particularly thinking about the Royal Docks, which is where we were when we had that meeting. He was talking about everything from building new homes to job creation, ultrafast internet, investment in infrastructure... Thinking about Stratford, *your* new home, the investment in infrastructure there is kind of unparalleled. It's one of the most connected places in the capital and Clive would talk about what the ripple of that looked like. Interestingly, Newham didn't have a cultural strategy until 2022 [ten years after the Olympic Games]. At the time when Clive and I met, the mayor there was Sir Robin Wales and he wasn't interested in arts and culture in the way that the current mayor, Rokhsana Fiaz, is. And it was really this conversation, and thinking about what the future could look like, and talking to him about what it could look like *outside* the Olympic Park, that kicked things off. You have these areas that are the focus of extraordinary amounts of investment – Queen Elizabeth Olympic Park, the Royal Docks, Greenwich Peninsula – but I guess what excited both of us was thinking about, creating connections, how you connect places, how you connect people to places, and what that means.

Clive was always interested in ideas and I asked if he would be interested if I could think of an idea that was compatible with all the things that he was talking about and he said, 'of course'. The idea I proposed was to take existing works of art – sculptures – that were in storage, and bring them outdoors, into an environment where everyone could enjoy them for free. We used to refer to the project as 'inside out'. It was a simple idea. But then we had to start thinking about how we could actually realise it. An idea that sounded quite simple, inevitably wasn't.

GCH And could you give us a sense of Newham? Because it is a very distinctive, particular place and that it had, as you say, even by that point in 2013, a significant amount of investment. And there are ways in which you can walk the length of a block and see both aspects of huge, positive change, but also areas that seem like they are being overlooked. And I know that it remains, in terms of all of those kinds of concerning metrics, one of the wards, one of the areas, one of the boroughs of deepest concern.

MP You're right. The structural inequalities and historic underinvestment in the area present a real, persistent challenge to overcome. To make sure that the investment that's now happening actually improves the lives of all the communities there is vital. As an area, it's one of the most culturally diverse in London, in fact the country. It also has a large young population. There is an opportunity for creating connections, giving people ways into areas that they may not have felt were accessible, and The Line – the spirit of The Line – is about democratising access to art. By creating a project that is connecting places and creating a journey – an experience, I guess – in its way, is an attempt to break down some of those barriers and increase access to art and nature.

GCH Which is ambitious and it's absolutely needed and kind of glorious. But at the same time, in that period of people thinking what the Olympic legacy would be, did you and Clive working together feel that this was something that spoke both to the spirit of the Olympics but also spoke to the need?

MP Yes. I think there was, and to some degree still is, a sense that the Olympic Park isn't for everyone. The nature of The Line is to create pathways, entry points to experiencing the local environment, to try to get people away from heavily trafficked roads, dense urban environments, to spend time next to water. And there's something magical about how the energy of a place changes when you get to the water. The Line is like a tributary, leading people to some of the places that might feel exclusive or alienating, offering a route that people can use as part of a commute to school, or to work … or for leisure. It gives a sense of connection and allows people to experience art on their own terms and in a way that's really meaningful to them.

GCH And also, that the creation of a sense of place, that this is an area which has had huge investment and shifts in the infrastructure, and with it, communities have changed. And there is natural churn, but there has been engineered change as well on top of that. And then, how one actually creates within and around and through that, something that speaks to the continuity, to the cultural DNA of that place, but also creates a sense of what a future spirit of that particular landscape might be. That was complex and were those things in your mind?

MP Yes, absolutely. Regeneration is really complicated. Newham's tagline was, and I think still is, 'A place to live, work and stay'. And the reality is, if you want people to stay in a place, you have to create a place that they want to be and somewhere they can afford to stay. And the idea of a place to stay was something that Clive and I reflected on a lot. With a transient population, how do you keep people there? And the River Lea, in particular, and the canal network around The Line is one of the area's great assets. Newham has such poor access to green space but the blue spaces are wonderful, and reflecting on the wellbeing benefits of spending time next to water, and the contemplative space that it offers, was a big part of our thinking.

GCH And how did you decide on the route of The Line?

MP Before Clive retired from the council, he got colleagues to take a map of the borough and drop 'pins' in locations that would be suitable for large outdoor sculpture. And it was looking at that, and realising that a lot of the locations were next to water, that we landed on the route. Originally, the project was going to be focused solely within Newham, and it was through conversations with the GLA [Greater London Authority] that we decided to extend the proposed route into Greenwich, using the cable car as the connection over the River Thames. And that also allowed us to think about including Antony Gormley and Richard Wilson's works, which were commissioned for the Millennium. Clive spent time in Accra, in Ghana, in 2013 and this got him thinking about the route we were talking about in Newham and the connection with the Greenwich Meridian. He coined the name – The Line – referencing that connection, and the route running north-south. Of course, The Line only broadly follows the Greenwich Meridian – it's not literally a straight line – but I think his ambition would've been for us to create a whole circumference…

GCH Oh, really? A circumference of the globe? That would be amazing.

MP Amazing, conceptually! I guess an idea that was already quite ambitious, became more so through its extension to Greenwich. I've tried to honour his ambition to connect with Accra through our *Longitudinal Dialogues* programme, which I'm sure we'll talk about later.

GCH And then, the loss of Clive [who passed away two weeks after The Line opened], at that point, did you ever think, 'maybe this is a project that is a wonderful kind of dream but I can step away…'? Or were you thinking, in terms of the memory of Clive, and the idea that you had conceived together, that you wanted to then do it all the more?

MP It was really hard after losing Clive. We were a great team and a brilliant, if slightly unlikely, double act. We shared an unwavering optimism, a belief in big ideas, and he had an infectious enthusiasm that always inspired people. I could never have set up The Line without Clive but I don't think he could have set up The Line without me

Mark Wallinger, Megan Piper and Clive Dutton at the Royal Docks, February 2014

either. There was a sort of mutual dependency on each other's skills and experiences that enabled the project to happen. The two of us used to go to meetings and there was a wonderful rapport between us and, for whatever reason, that dynamic, we worked so well together. And when he died … well, I felt a terrible sense of loss, but also a sense of responsibility, knowing that The Line was part of his legacy. There was also a moment when I wasn't sure that I could do it without him, and it all felt too much, and I wanted to hand over the project, but, ultimately, I didn't. I think the spirit of The Line, its essence, has always been about people. That's why it started and that's why it's got to this point ten years on. Clive and I appealed to people for help, to get involved, to make connections, and that's what I've continued to do. At the beginning, though, it required a real leap of faith. We were just two people with an idea and…

GCH A good idea, though.

MP A good idea, which I think helped. But it was just that – an idea. We used to go to meetings and ask people if they wanted to come and join us. And the team grew through the two of us reaching out to people we knew and having lots of conversations with lots of different people. And one of the first people that I spoke to was [the architect] Ivan Harbour who is still involved with the project to this day.

GCH How wonderful.

MP I interviewed Ivan and [the late architect] Richard Rogers when we were crowdfunding. They thought The Line was an exciting proposition, and the fact that it would be open to everybody was really important. And RSHP, as a practice, has been on board since 2014, completing our planning applications, supporting through their foundation, and Ivan's now a trustee … We had an early group of supporters that included [the artist] Mark Wallinger, and it was their collective belief in the project that helped to give it its momentum. Without their collective support, we would never have got The Line off the ground. I was in a meeting with a colleague some time ago, who said that 'The Line brings out the best in people'. I think it's that sense that has allowed the project to develop in the way it has.

And in terms of losing Clive, it was also really hard because his world was so very different to mine. I'd never done anything in the public realm. He understood how local government works, the GLA, what the landscape looked like in terms of Newham's future, the property developers and their developments ... That wasn't my world.

GCH But doesn't that make it all the more commendable, that you had this intellectual, this visionary kind of DNA that you had created in collaboration with Clive, then despite the loss of him that you have managed to negotiate the development of something that feels very much like it's been delivered in the spirit of what he envisioned.

MP I hope so. If he could see us sat here, on the eve of our tenth anniversary, I think he'd be thrilled. And proud of what The Line's become. Clive really believed that you could do things, change things, and his work was rooted in a commitment to improving the quality of life for people in urban environments.

GCH It's a fitting legacy for someone who's committed so much to the area and to the things that we all love. In a way, it is one of the great Olympic legacies because the spirit of the Olympics is about excellence and also inclusion. And I think that's what is manifest in The Line, that this is the incredible exemplification of how the arts can draw communities together, raise spirits and raise awareness and get people involved.

MP I hope that's what we do! I think there was something like 70,000 volunteers who participated in the Olympics, and that sense of community and pride, it was important to think about how we might be able to build on that. I know in the conversation you had with [former Olympic British track and field athlete, and Newham resident] Christine Ohuruogu [for our Walking and Talking podcast about the legacy of the Olympics], you talked about Rio and what, in comparison, it's like there. And I've been to Sydney ... And you look at what's happening in the Olympic Park *here* and it's...

GCH It's extraordinary.

MP It is extraordinary. And when I do tours of The Line and take people to the Park and tell them about what's happening with East Bank – yourselves [V&A East], BBC Music, London College of Fashion, UCL East, Sadler's Wells – it's amazing. It certainly lives up to what Clive would've wanted it to be.

GCH That's wonderful.

MP The route of The Line connects so many different, interesting places, though. Clive introduced me to Cody Dock, which I always cite as the most inspiring example of community-led regeneration. They've had something like 18,000 volunteers through their doors, clearing the site of waste, building everything from community gardens to an outdoor classroom, studios, they have a café, the most amazing rolling bridge – a true feat of engineering – they grow vegetables, keep bees ... And they have a vibrant programme of events too, including an event where you can drink beer and count bats! There are many things that tap into the history and heritage of the area, and involving people in the development, taking them on a journey, is what it's all about.

Cody Dock's Rolling Bridge, designed by Thomas Randall-Page

GCH And in a way, that sense of journey, not just across geography but also across time, is what The Line links. But could you tell us a little bit about the journey of the development of The Line that we talked about in that initial period with Clive? There are some really innovative things that you did around funding, and can you talk a little bit about some of those initial projects? Just to get a sense of, not just what an incredible project it is, but how innovative it has been as well.

MP We crowdfunded to get us started and used a civic crowdfunding platform called Spacehive. And crowdfunding, in terms of the democratisation of fundraising, felt really important, that it chimed with the whole approach that we were taking to the project. I'd never crowdfunded, Clive had never crowdfunded, and we were extremely naïve when we started that campaign. We were trying to raise over £140,000 to initiate the project and tied the campaign to Valentine's Day [2014]. And the messaging we had was, 'If you love London, love The Line'. The entry level for pledges was £2 and we originally gave ourselves eleven days to meet our target [this was later extended to six weeks].

Sarah Sands was the editor of the *Evening Standard* at that time and we had great coverage around the campaign launch. We had this idea that bringing everyone together, to be part of it, was really what The Line was about. We listed people's donations in the order that they pledged. So if you gave £2 before someone else gave £200, your name was higher on the list. The idea was that you could give at a relatively low level, but that that mattered, and people should feel empowered to give.

GCH Because so regularly within the arts, you go into a big institution and the donors, the supporters are named and usually ranked in terms of how much they contribute.

MP Exactly.

GCH And then what you are saying is thinking about how do you democratise?

MP Yes, it was about speed and not money. So the faster you gave, the higher your name was. And at the same time that we crowdfunded, we also did an open call for works of art – loans – for artists, galleries and private collectors to propose work for inclusion in The Line's programme. Works that were considered by a panel. And again, that idea of opening it up and inviting...

GCH And quality, because so often there are conservative commentators who grow concerned that, by opening up and democratising things, that you can, in some way, compromise the quality or the vision. But did you find that was the case?

MP No, I think that we always held onto the ambition, or a commitment, to present ... I don't know, well, whatever you want to call it: 'museum-quality' or 'world-class' work. But then we had the selected works, but without specific locations for them, and had the challenge...

GCH Of finding the right settings.

MP Exactly. Finding locations, where you have a pre-selected group, trying to place them along The Line in a way that ... resonates.

GCH And did that require negotiation with the artists as well?

MP Yes, the artists, or their representatives, generally came to view the proposed sites. I remember visiting Greenwich Peninsula with [artist] Gary Hume and [curator] Andrea Schlieker, who was working at White Cube at the time, and she had commissioned Antony Gormley and Richard Wilson's works for the Millennium, and I remember how daunting that was, being there with her and Gary, presenting a site for approval. And I think we were so mindful of people's experience of The Line, not wanting them to feel like works had been 'plonked' along the route. It was a really tough thing to curate once the works had been selected. But I think that, overall, we were successful with it. And there are three works [by Thomson & Craighead, Gary Hume and Abigail Fallis] that were part of that inaugural open call that are still on the route today, nearly ten years later.

GCH And one of your inaugural loans in 2015 was a work by Thomas J Price who is creating an eighteen-foot-high work that will be installed outside V&A East in the spring of 2026, and we are hoping that this will be just the beginning of a number of public realm interventions that in many ways lean upon your work. And we are hoping that they will be artists that represent the shared values of V&A East and The Line ...

MP It's really exciting to think about that commission and what it will mean. Certainly, *Network* – and later, *Reaching Out* – had such a profound effect on local audiences, including former Youth Guides who still reflect on it. There's a considerable amount to do to improve representation within the public realm, and Thomas has been a leading light in this space. I'm proud that, now, over 50 per cent of artists on the route [commissioned by The Line] are women, which is something we expect to maintain. And, assuming all projects that are currently in development proceed, we expect that just under 50 per cent will be artists of colour by the end of 2026.

GCH And just so that I understand the route, which is defined by these amazing works, the works can change over a period of time?

MP Yes, the works change. Queen Elizabeth Olympic Park and The O2 have always been the 'bookends' of the route but, within that route, the works change. There are currently around twenty-five installations on The Line, including five works that The Line wasn't involved in commissioning. They're permanent anchors, as it were. So that's Antony Gormley, Richard Wilson, Anish Kapoor, Carsten Höller ... and Alex Chinneck, whose work is semi-permanent and due to be deinstalled later this year. We've agreed with those artists that their works are part of The Line.

It's funny, I watched our crowdfunding video in anticipation of this conversation and was reminded that our original intention was to have thirty works installed on The Line for three years. With an idea that we would repeat the [open call] process again three years later. But the way the programme has actually developed has been much more dynamic. When it came to it, we could only borrow works for an initial period of two years. That was what lenders felt they could commit to. They couldn't agree to three years and, for us – from a cost point of view – it didn't make sense to have them for less. So, loans initially come to us for two years and then, where they've stayed, they've been extended by mutual agreement. In 2020, we launched our first sound commission [with Larry Achiampong] and since then, we have started inviting artists to create site-specific works for The Line.

GCH So it has been like having an external gallery, that you've actually curated those spaces and organically adapted to opportunity and changing relationships with the artists and the space. And it's such a complex set of demands from so many. And how have you balanced those? And also, I imagine that there are planning and local authority needs and there are all sorts of issues with thinking about engineering and structures and setting and location and all of those other things, and maintenance. All of that stuff.

MP I had no idea when I started!

GCH I know. Because I began that list and I just thought, 'Oh my word, how is it?' You must be a superwoman. I just have no idea how you've done it.

MP I think it's like so many things, if you knew what it would take to do something, you might not do it. In fact, we originally thought that we could open The Line in 2014, after reaching our crowdfunding target and raising additional funds, but we successfully demonstrated that it is beyond human capability to conceive of a public art project and launch it in London within one year. It's just not possible. The Line connects three local authorities – Newham, Tower Hamlets and Greenwich – and we've had to work with four planning authorities because the Olympic Park and the surrounding area is run by the London Legacy Development Corporation. And then land ownership; The Line doesn't own any land, so every installation requires negotiation with a landowner. Of course, engineering requirements are a massive consideration and we're lucky that Arup have come on board as supporters over recent years, and we've co-curated a number of projects with their Head of Cultural Heritage and Exhibitions, Jennifer Greitschus. We've also needed a lot of cranes!

GCH And then, all those boring things like insurance and maintenance...

MP Absolutely. It's so important that we look after the installations. And, actually, if people can see that works are cared for, they tend to look after them. Graffiti attracts graffiti, and as soon as something's seen to be neglected, it can become a magnet for vandalism ... We have an art technician now who condition checks works, cleans them, and there is a sort of community policing that goes on as well. So, in the very few instances that there have been incidents of malicious damage, things have been reported pretty promptly. But touch wood...

GCH It's amazing.

MP We've been pretty lucky.

GCH But that does speak to this project having been really well considered. What kind of work have you done with communities to make sure that, when these works were sited, people didn't feel like they were just kind of being dropped from outer space and that they were alien and they could reject them, couldn't they? They might be resistant to the whole scheme, they might feel this was part of some sort of gentrification. There are all kinds of ways in which communities have responded negatively to public art. And I'm just wondering how you've actually managed to deal with that.

MP In the early days, when Clive and I were setting it up, we used to visit all sorts of community groups, from Community Links to library groups, as well as other community organisations, like the Peacock Gym down by the Royal Docks and places like the House Mill, who are still part of our route and programme. And when we selected

Installation of Abigail Fallis, *DNA DL90* in 2015 (above), and deinstallation of Damien Hirst, *Sensation* in 2019

the inaugural loans, Simon Myers, who runs Cody Dock, joined the selection panel as a community representative. We talked to a lot of people. And more recently, we've been doing a lot to develop programmes that allow local communities to build a sense of ownership of The Line.

GCH Can you say a bit more about that?

MP So we started commissioning work in 2020, and in 2021 we launched our first multi-site exhibition of works by Madge Gill, *Nature in Mind*, co-curated with Sophie Dutton, Clive's daughter. It was a wonderful opportunity to build on Clive's ambition to present Madge Gill's work within Newham, the borough where she spent most of her life, and to give people who live locally a sense of connection to the works that are owned by the local authority. We reproduced a series of drawings from the Council's collection, which includes around 1,200 works donated by her family when she died. It felt really important to open Newham's collection to the community and to raise awareness of her practice. Her works range in scale, from postcards to vast calicos, and there's an amazing photograph of Madge Gill in her garden, taken in 1947, showing how she would bring her largest works outdoors, to see them in their entirety (see page 18). And I think this photograph makes sense of the approach we took to the exhibition, reflecting a process that she engaged with in her own lifetime. When she was in her thirties, Madge Gill was seen by the psychiatrist Helen Boyle, who went on to set up the mental health charity, Mind. When we launched the exhibition, we developed an engagement programme with service users from a local Mind centre, culminating in an exhibition of workshop outcomes at Stratford Library.

GCH And more recently, I think you've started co-commissioning works?

MP Yes, we were awarded funding from Newham Council to deliver three new public art commissions. Through this, we have expanded our curatorial approach to include co-commissioning and have recruited people from the local community to work with us. We did a flyer drop to residents

Madge Gill hanging one of her works in her garden in East Ham, assisted by her son, Lawrence, 19 August 1947.
The 1.8 x 11 m piece is made from ink on calico and is Gill's largest work to date

who are local to Cody Dock, essentially a call-out to people to put themselves forward to be part of the project, as well as promoting the opportunity on our social media. The co-commissioners worked with us for about eighteen months, were paid the London Living Wage, researched the area, prepared briefs for the artists and ultimately selected which artist to appoint for each commission.

GCH But what was the initial response? Was this something that seemed to excite those that heard about it?

MP I think *intrigue* was probably the initial, overarching response. We understood that not everyone would like everything and that, actually, that's not the role of public art. Stimulating dialogue and people connecting with something – positively or negatively – is important. It's taken a while for people to think about The Line as a curated programme, rather than a series of isolated installations, and I think the idea of the route as a whole has taken longer to come together in people's minds.

GCH So, tell me about that element, then. Because I've come to understand the politics that surrounded it, the origins of it, the way in which you've dealt with all of the planning and local authority constraints, and then, the way in which you've engaged with artists, a sense that you created a really fantastic bedrock for what you're about to deliver. And then, how did you begin to conceive a sense of the narrative of The Line, the communications around The Line, the sense of the identity of this project?

MP Our earliest engagement project post-launch was

with the House of Fairy Tales, who developed a learning resource that focused on the layers of The Line and its educational potential, focusing on the route as a place where people can discover art, nature and heritage for free. The work we started with them was the beginning of telling that story and engaging with schools. Thinking about The Line as an outdoor classroom for cross-curricular learning – and how to connect with young people in a meaningful way – is something that we've been building on, and we'll continue to build on as the organisation grows. But it's only in the last few years that we've had a dedicated engagement team and the capacity to expand this aspect of our work.

For years after Clive died, there were really just two of us, me and Charlotte [Booth]. And in 2019, Sarah [Carrington] joined the team. And actually, it was her experience with commissioning that led to the expansion of our programming and also our fundraising capacity. In 2020, in the throes of the pandemic, we marked our fifth anniversary with the launch of new works by Larry Achiampong and Thomas J Price, and significant investment in our digital presence, including the launch of our digital guide on Bloomberg Connects. In 2022, the team grew from three to eleven. And it's through the team and their ideas and vision that the programme has developed in the way it has.

GCH And how are you working with communities now?

MP We now have a learning programme that's much more developed, and a team focused on that, working with primary and secondary schools, as well as university partnerships that look at the impact of our work. And we have a wellbeing programme that we've developed where people can be referred to us by their GP or social prescribing link worker. We have a weekly wellbeing walk, as well as walks and workshops that we deliver annually for people living with early-stage dementia. And then one of the really key things, just going back to earlier thoughts about the legacy of the Olympics, is job creation, and thinking about the work we're doing around youth employment, creating opportunities for young people as well as thinking about how to demystify creative career pathways. That's one of the things I'm proudest of. We now have our annual Youth Guides programme that employs about twenty-five eighteen to twenty-one-year-olds every summer. We train them, they're paid the London Living Wage, and they stand in pairs along the route every weekend, engaging the public in conversation about The Line. And in terms of developing a sense of ownership of The Line, that has been one of the most important projects, which has had an enduring impact on people. Every year, we re-employ previous Youth Guides as Supervisors, so there's a professional development opportunity too. We've got young people who've now been working with us for four years, coming back and co-facilitating engagement projects. And offering a way for young people to come on the journey with us, and be part of it, has been brilliant. Also, having local representation within the team, but also on the board, has been important. We've really worked to recruit trustees who have a local connection to The Line...

GCH Very nice. And that sense of continuity that, over the course of the story of The Line, which in itself is kind of an investment in narrative, the loss of colleagues, of Clive, the loss of friends, as you say, people like Richard Rogers, who we've lost along the way. But then, the growth of your team, of this Line family. And then, as you go forward, an investment in young people and a new generation. Can you tell me a little bit about what you foresee as the next steps and how you will engage a younger generation in not just becoming part of The Line, but in re-conceiving The Line for a new generation?

MP I think there are a few things to reflect on in terms of thinking about the future and I probably need to break down the question into two parts. Firstly, perhaps, it feels like the right moment to acknowledge that we've recently announced that I'm standing down as Director of The Line and that my deputy, Sarah, has been appointed as my successor. This feels like a massive step for the organisation. It's amazing to think that it's now so much bigger than me, that it has a life of its own, and that it will continue to grow under someone else's leadership.

GCH And the future, I know that is important to you...?

MP Very important. We've got the foundations to build on in terms of our co-commissioning model. Our Youth Collective actually visited the V&A and your ironworks collection as part of our project with Mahtab Hussain – the culmination of a three-year collaboration with the National Portrait Gallery and London College of Fashion. The project reflects on the representation of young people in the digital and public realms. The commissioned work is a bench in the Olympic Park, a prop for portraiture, that creates space for people to engage, to take photographs of themselves and each other, and to post them on social media, celebrating creativity and thinking about what it means to be a young person in East London.

GCH Well, that connects the ambition of Clive and yourself at the beginning, and that sense of continuity and the way in which you are passing on some of this to young people in terms of opportunity, in terms of thinking about the future of this place that is changing so quickly.

MP A nice project to reflect on is the one I mentioned earlier, *Longitudinal Dialogues*, that relates to Clive's ambition to connect The Line in London with Accra. In 2022, we commissioned the Ghanaian artist Serge Attukwei Clottey to create an installation at Greenwich Peninsula. Clive actually met Serge in Accra in 2013. And alongside the commission, we developed an engagement programme that connected six primary schools in Newham with six in Accra, culminating in a procession in each city. It was the most extraordinary day and I hope it's an experience that will stay with those children forever (see image below).

And it goes back to the point about people, and creating an experience, and through that experience and people sharing it, becoming ambassadors for The Line. One of the things about The Line is that it satisfies the yearning people have for new experiences. Once we get people to The Line and they experience it, it's something that stays with them. And no two visits to The Line are the same. Between the changing weather, the tides … Of course, the rivers are heavily tidal, so if you're there at high tide or low tide, it feels like a completely different landscape. And that dynamic nature means that once people have been, they generally don't forget it. I see people who I walked The Line with ten years ago, and they say that they still talk about it. I think that that experience, and that sense of connection that people have, they take with them. And going back to the starting point with Clive, where it all began, was about connecting people … people spreading the word and raising awareness in a very organic way.

GCH And driving that with integrity and humility. Because I think that there are other similar projects in the world that perhaps have been undone by hubris. And I do think, in a way, the embeddedness of this and the integrity of it is something that means that, over the course of a decade, it feels every bit as resonant and as right as it did when I first heard about it a decade ago. And I think that speaks to your original vision, but also the strength that you have in your team of maintaining that vision.

MP I feel lucky to have such a brilliant team and am so happy that Sarah will lead The Line into its second decade. And I often think of … well, two things. One is that, if somebody came to me, or came to the team, with the idea

Procession at Greenwich Peninsula led by Serge Attukwei Clottey and One-Drum Foundation

of starting another version of The Line with a really, really large pot of money, you wouldn't be able to create The Line. I think the fact that Clive and I started it with nothing more than an idea, and how it's grown from something that we cooked up over coffee to where it is today, it wouldn't be what it is if someone had written us a cheque for five million pounds on day one. You couldn't create it. You couldn't create The Line with just money. We needed goodwill and for people to invest their belief in us.

The second thing is that even if Clive were alive today, I don't think we could set up The Line today. In terms of its geography, where it is and what it is, and on the eve of the full opening of East Bank, I don't think you could start it now. I think we were in the right place, at the right time, having the right conversation. That's enabled it to become what it is. Conversations take so long to develop and the landscape has changed so much over these years. Of course, there's you [V&A East] there, English National Ballet at London City Island, the Design District at Greenwich Peninsula.

GCH And what do you think of us newcomers?

MP Oh, it's fantastic! How exciting to think about East Bank at the top of The Line. Providing a place for people to explore, to discover, to learn. The UK's newest cultural quarter.

GCH I personally think it's a beautiful natural terminus for The Line in terms of its geography, and it's a coming together of many of the imperatives and drivers that you have been concerned with in a number of institutions. So, I think it works really well in terms of geography and vision coming together.

MP I think so too. Collaboration is at the heart of how we work, and for me, I look and see the opportunity that's there for collaboration, the development of interdisciplinary dialogue, bringing together partners to develop innovative ways of working, pushing the boundaries of what public art can do. When we started The Line, we had our loans programme and, generally, presented works of a certain scale, but now, thinking about how things don't have to be big to be powerful, how we can create site-specific work collaboratively, that's really exciting. When we commissioned Larry Achiampong to create *Sanko-time*, we were thinking about how you can think creatively within the public realm and do things differently. To create something that is inspiring and has impact, is unique and brings people together, has got to be what it's all about.

GCH Well, I think that's a perfect sense on which to end. We at the V&A and the East Bank family are absolutely delighted to be there on site and aware of some of this history, this incredible history and heritage that has been built by people who have made such a profound contribution to shaping the landscape of this part of London. And within that is the integrity of projects like yours that don't just help us to redefine geography and our sense of community, but also have helped us to understand how public art can be more than just a way marker. How it can actually become a kind of spiritual focus for communities and set the bar high so that institutions like ours, when we come to join you in communities like East London, that we can have an understanding of both the past, but how that can very powerfully inform the future. And not just of our institutions, but of the communities that we all serve.

YOU ARE HERE
JES FERNIE

Let's start here, where you are standing, sitting, looking, hunching, breathing. This is the beginning. Throw yourself into a crisp winter's day at the end of the first quarter of the twenty-first century. It's late afternoon, the sun casts enormous greedy shadows over the landscape around you. We are in North Greenwich, an area in south-east London that conjures images of majestic excess, ships, architectural grandeur, and a dictatorial relationship to the constructs of time. You can see your breath ahead of you as you begin to walk towards the river, that bit that forms a magnificent U and is framed by the Isle of Dogs, where Henry VIII kept his canine friends. To the east of here lies the truncated runway of London City Airport, from where the world stretches out ad infinitum. A black-headed gull squawks overhead, gliding towards a place that doesn't involve you; a cyclist rushes past, smiling at something you can't see. There's the hum of industry: construction sites, cranes in motion, ventilation shafts, twenty-first-century white noise – all folded into a rich, fraught history of shipbuilding and dock work. A man wearing a lanyard appears on the other side of a fence; he looks like he's daydreaming, not working. There are closed ecosystems here that are self-sufficient and mute; but there are others that invite you in, pointing towards past and future possibilities and things unknown, posing questions, proposing answers, issuing provocations.

Some of these generous, open systems take the form of artworks, installed by the river, over the river, on the river, on railings, walkways and buildings, from North Greenwich to Stratford. Together, they suggest ways of relating to the world, to ourselves, and things we have built up around us. I want to say that they, and the environment in which they sit, inspire a kind of epiphany, but that sounds too grand for an experience in which you are not the main actor.

At the top of a pole, on this walkway at the tip of Greenwich Peninsula, there's an unprepossessing municipal road sign that reads 'Here 24,859'. It is an artwork by Alison Craighead and Jon Thomson that locates you in space and informs you, in a beautifully concise manner, that if you were to travel around the earth to arrive back at yourself, you will have travelled 24,859 miles. I'm thinking of my daughter as a baby, crawling up the stairs for the first time, glancing back at me, grinning with toothless pride. I realised that I'd been conceiving of her life as a set of future possibilities (What will she become? How will she relate to the world?) and now understood that she is what she is now, here, in this moment, and this is what matters. And here I am, twenty-four years later, thinking of it again, reflecting on our need to construct narratives using time and distance as tools to build our worlds and tether us to life.

I walk on, my hands increasingly numb with cold, watching three men fix a puncture in a bike tire. They are in good spirits; their Lycra-clad bodies suggest that they aren't in a hurry, there's nothing urgent to get to. I come across a section of ship that has been bolted into the riverbed. Installed to celebrate the Millennium twenty-five years ago, this is Richard Wilson's sublime offering to the maritime gods, *A Slice of Reality*: an ocean sand dredger called the Arco Trent that he cut through to reveal the innards. I can see bits of ramshackle furniture, a faded album cover placed up against the window (is that the chiselled face of Feargal Sharkey surveying the water quality below?), and pipes that no longer provide a function beyond intrigue. This hulking great object that is so easy to miss unless you are told to see it, alludes to the violence of the Meridian line. Forged 140 years ago to prop up a universal understanding of time, it helps us cut across the specificities of cultures and lives with effortless indifference and criminal insensitivity. This artwork tethers us to a history of empire that is both painful and significant. It is ageing alongside us and gets more ragged and complex every year. A friend messages to tell me that she called the mobile number posted on a hand-painted wooden plaque on the section of ship. The artist picked up.

Detail: Richard Wilson's *A Slice of Reality* at Greenwich Peninsula

They had a great chat, she said. This is a special kind of public offering. The art, the artist, the history, the light, the thing.

The river is a constant companion for much of this walk. It is murky and dense, light glancing off its silvery surface. It is famously hard to photograph, and, like anything worth its salt, it has a strong undercurrent. It holds a multitude of secrets. I read somewhere that before Phyllida Barlow was *the* Phyllida Barlow she would – under cover of darkness – throw her sculptures into the Thames because she couldn't afford to store them. So there's art down there, as well as bits of old pottery, bottle tops, coins, shopping trollies, bones and bodies. On average (it says here, in my phantasmic AI-facilitated online search), a human body is found in the Thames once a fortnight. That's a lot of violence, misery, secrets and shadows. This collection of human effluence is accompanied by rats and seals, eels and seahorses, leafy-dragons and sharks. Myriad fantastical creatures inhabit this underworld. From the corner of my mind's eye, I see the ghosts of pirates who were hanged at Wapping, whose bodies were grimly displayed along the peninsula as a deterrent to those considering similar acts of extraction by stealth.

Not far up from Wilson's dredger, I find *Tribe and Tribulation*, Serge Attukwei Clottey's totemic sculpture, and am transported from my dark piratical reverie to Accra, in Ghana, the only other capital city that sits on the prime meridian. Made from fragments of Ghanaian fishing boats, this majestic, towering structure emits the sound of activity in the former slave forts of Cape Coast Castle, Elmina Castle and James Fort: fishermen and women hustling, waves crashing, birds screeching, things clanking. These abandoned forts have been reclaimed through trade, migration, industrialisation, and a complex web of consumerism and inequality. If I squint into the light, I can see a procession of children weaving their way through the streets of Greenwich and Accra, wearing masks they have fashioned from discarded material, plastic bottles, cardboard, paint and fabric. They are dancing, chanting and banging drums, assuming fantastical characters in wild abandon. It feels like a tear in the time-space continuum has opened up and the children are inhabiting both cities at the same moment. Riverboats toot their horns, there is freedom and glee in the air; a sense of future possibilities and connectedness traversing the globe. Everyone, it seems, is smiling.[1]

This walking route lies on the margins of London. It is rough edgeland that speaks of lives lived in compromised, beautiful, bewildering complexity. It is haphazard, ragged, bolted together by the necessities of survival rather than some finely authored singular flourish. The neoliberalising property cadre have only partly moved in, dipping their toes in the river to gauge the temperature of their likely net profits. This frayed world is echoed in the wild, abstract drawings of self-taught, local artist Madge Gill (1882–1961), whose artwork is installed across five locations on The Line. At Cody Dock, the sun glances off a bridge that has been clad in a detail of one of her rich drawings, and on the walkway leading up

Procession at Greenwich Peninsula led by Serge Attukwei Clottey

to the dock there's a tender photograph of her wearing one of her multi-coloured, sculptural dresses. She is leaning against a baroque nineteenth-century cabinet that reeks of showy 'exoticism' and cares nothing for this frail, self-conscious old woman, with her parted grey hair, gnarled hands and downward glance. But how majestic and otherworldly she looks, wearing this dress that refuses the mores of contemporary life and embraces an inner world of imagination and play.

Gill's life was hard; she lived for a while in an orphanage as a child, survived on meagre resources, suffered from mental turmoil as a result of the death of two children, and received little public recognition for her work. She had a spirit guide called Myrninerest and used paint, inks and textiles to create thousands of drawings in which spiderwebs, faces, petals, buildings and chequerboards dance together in a kind of fraught ecstasy. In another photograph, sited further along the wall, there she is unravelling one of her huge eleven-metre calico drawings in her garden. Her floral shapes form a union with the light and plants of the natural world; it's an alchemical, strangely hopeful vision, made all the more poignant by the quality of the photograph's fading and the surrounding plant life of the dock. Madge Gill: remember her name. She's receiving her due now, more than half a century after her death, her ghost haunting an art historical canon that seems to take pride in its exclusion of people living on the edges.

When I walk over Simon Faithfull's thirty-eight paving stones that reference the 0° line of longitude, I think back to Wilson's ship and reflect on the absurdity and hubris of this carving of the globe into a series of parallel lines, how it created the necessary culture of time for building empires, and how that culture is still with us, embedded in our language, our institutions, the way we view the world, and the continued impoverishment and underdevelopment of supposedly *post*colonial states. Writer Giordano Nanni reminds us that 'clocks ... do not keep *the* time, but *a* time'[2] and Edward Said wrote about the West's dichotomy of West vs East, how these are 'ideological fictions ... constructs ... weapons of cultural war',[3] but he could just as easily be talking about time. It took me far too long to realise that the East is only the East if you are standing in the West. As a child, my parents had a Turkish world atlas that they kept on a shelf in the living room. The cloth cover was a dreamy Mediterranean Sea blue, and of course all the text, including country and city names, was Turkish. I realised, as an adult, I had navigated the early part of my life harbouring a hazy sense that the world was Turkish and that all other languages and countries were somehow a permitted concession to its otherwise hegemonic dominance. The irony! Of me with my British passport and all its accompanying privileges.

Along the walkway that takes me from Three Mills to Sugar House Island, I meet a man with a wildly enthusiastic little dog whose wagging tail seems to dictate the terms of his engagement. The man tells me that a car accident rendered him unable to work. He walks this segment of The Line every day; it has helped him piece things back together, he says. The artworks, the landscape, the sounds, the birds, the neighbours – they have all supported him along the way. I feel quite emotional thinking about the implications of all this, how important it is for us to be able to find places, things, people that are there for us when things fall apart, and how hard this is in a world that is increasingly fragmented, monetised, mined, hollowed out. The dog refuses my mawkishness and is busy greeting everyone who walks by with a proprietorial air. His owner smiles proudly and says: 'He thinks this is his garden and these people are just visitors.'

Recently, I have become interested in ways that we can mark time in relation to public artworks. These things that are in our lives over long periods, they can become barometers for gauging the rate of change all around, the ageing process, the shifting of a mindset or life-choices. We experience them with our bodies, our breath, our current reality, our daydreams, our perfectly strange, muffled attempts to map out our day and locate ourselves in the world. When I first saw Wilson's ship in the enthusiastic fanfare that was the Millennium, I was thirty-one. September 11 and the Iraq War had not yet happened and we were marching blithely past threats of a future climate catastrophe. I was old enough to recognise what I was becoming, but young enough to potentially misconstrue the narrative. Looking at *A Slice of Reality* now, I am able to somehow conjure an invisible, rich, knotted thread, that is both incredibly personal and fantastically universal, which stretches from the past to arrive at the present, nodding to a notional, unseeable future.

When we make friends with an artwork, it can be alarming when it disappears. There are many reasons why this might happen: damage, decay, destruction, a new home elsewhere, a finite lifespan. When Tracey Emin's tiny bronze birds were deinstalled from their location on the bank of the tidal River Lea, local people expressed their sorrow. Perched on top of slender poles, with a dramatic backdrop that encompassed the world's largest surviving tidal mill, these fragile little characters seemed to look out for us all, chattering to each other across the airwaves. During COVID, a local woman took solace in the sculpture, titled *A Moment Without You*, reflecting on the recent deaths of family members. I imagine that she was sad to see the birds go. This mourning of an absent artwork is a powerful reminder of our own mortality as well as the importance of valuing something in the moment, but most beguilingly, it can teach us that a void can be more insistent and 'real' than something in its embodied state. I'm hoping that the site that once held *A Moment Without You* becomes an ongoing space for expansive reflection. I often think about the fact that thousands of people queued for hours to see the space left by the stolen *Mona Lisa* at the Louvre in 1911. There's a blurry black-and-white photograph of packed crowds fiercely studying a dusty wall. The emptiness that marks the absence of an artwork can take root in our imagination and assume a chameleon-like narrative that bends to suit the occasion, the storyteller or the revised context. It poses the idea that perhaps we can see something more clearly when it's not there.

We have reached Queen Elizabeth Olympic Park at Stratford, the end of The Line, which is the beginning for many. It is dark; we emerge into the noise, the lights, the people, the movement of city life. The fledgling waterfront development at East Bank, constructed on the foundations of London's 2012 Olympian endeavour, as well as centuries of toil by brewers, potato farmers and weavers, is setting down roots, testing its relation to the rest of the city. I'm not entirely ready for this reintroduction, but I'm taking this gift, this folding and unravelling of time, and the dreaming of artists, to shore up my reserves, to make future things possible.

1 On 26 May 2022, children in Accra and London took part in simultaneous processions, the culmination of a school programme in each city initiated by The Line and funded by the British Council, inspired by Serge Attukwei Clottey's practice.
2 *The Colonisation of Time*, Giordano Nanni, Manchester University Press, 2013.
3 *Orientalism*, Edward Said, Pantheon Books, 1978.

PEOPLE
ANDREW JONES

Art gallery, school route, commute. Nature reserve, employer, park. Safe space, classroom, gym. Place of healing, learning and village green. The Line touches people in many different ways.

Public engagement begins even before a work is made or installed. Niyi Abidakun, a data analyst who lives near The Line, had always been intrigued by graffiti and 'legal' public art, trying to fathom the meaning of pieces he passed on his way to work: How did they get there? What were they saying? As a local of Canning Town, he was also proud of his neighbourhood – 'My Manor' – and how it was developing. One day he chanced upon an advertisement on Instagram: The Line was looking for co-commissioners for a new work across an existing cable bridge. He was selected and in the first meeting felt as if he had been 'let loose' as he and his co-commissioners debated what would make a great piece of public art. Over the course of eight months, the group went from a long list to a short list before selecting Helen Cammock to produce a text-based piece. To help with the selection process, Niyi used his analytics background to devise a rigorous scoring system based on the criteria the group had come up with.

'We helped create a proper artwork. Not something that gets scrubbed off. Not ASBO [antisocial behaviour order] art, like graffiti.' Accessibility was crucial for Niyi. 'The only way you can't access Helen's piece is if you can't read. And that's a different problem.' The accessibility of the work is connected to the physical accessibility of this part of London. 'Before the Olympics, you had to be either a bandit or a son of the soil to go there. Now the area is open to everyone from kids to pensioners.' For Niyi, the experience was transformative; having been at the heart of the commission, he said, 'I cannot go back into the world as an art civilian now.'

Helen Cammock (above), and Niyi Abidakun on the River Lea before and after the installation of *On WindTides*

Mahtab Hussain (above left) on *Please Take a Seat* in Queen Elizabeth Olympic Park, and Amar Lodhia, and his dog Pepe, outside the House Mill

Local engagement also underpins Mahtab Hussain's work, *Please Take a Seat*, a cast iron park bench. The Line's Youth Collective (whose members' portraits are incorporated into the backrest) helped Mahtab identify elements of local history and tradition for incorporation into the bench's design: from jellied eels to grime music, abstract Islamic motifs to the local grey heron. 'For many, the Olympic Park is a brand-new place – structures by Zaha Hadid, Anish Kapoor and Carsten Höller, the giant shopping centre [Westfield] and all the new housing around it. But it is also a part of London with centuries of history, deep local culture. The bench bridges the modern world with this history,' said Mahtab.

The engagement continues beyond its installation. The bench invites people to 'activate' it with their thoughts and views on social media. 'Making and installing the work is just the beginning,' explained Mahtab. 'I want this work to have a life of its own, fashioned by its users.' Niyi agreed: 'Community art should linger, change, evolve.'

The Line also changes with the climate and the time of day. Amar Lodhia, who lives locally, has been walking The Line every day for almost two years. 'The art varies with the seasons, the weather, and even my own state of mind, so every walk feels unique.' Amar has been recovering from the physical and mental effects of a car crash. A convert to Buddhism, Amar uses The Line for meditation and mindful walking. 'The art naturally invites you to slow down, observe and engage with your surroundings.' Each sculpture or installation 'offers a new perspective, a moment to pause and reflect. Sometimes, I'll focus on a piece and simply observe it without judgement, which is a core part of mindfulness. The Line is a daily ritual for me.'

Catherine Sizer participates in The Line's weekly Wellbeing Walks, having lost her partner of thirty-seven years. These weekly sessions take different forms: water meditation, in which you might contemplate the ripples and the colours of the canal ('Sometimes it is a deep olive green,' marvelled Catherine); dancing on the embankment; breathing exercises; as well as outings to pottery classes, local allotments or the Stepney City Farm. In between the weekly sessions, she takes photographs and paints watercolours of The Line, appreciating the 'beauty of different weather'. 'The Line is the only nice thing that has happened since David died.'

The Line crosses three demographically textured boroughs (Greenwich, Newham and Tower Hamlets), a complicated mix of brand-new residential developments in previously industrial settings, and areas with long-standing structural inequalities, grouping an extraordinary range of cultures and ethnicities (over 100 languages are spoken in Newham alone). Population transience figures are high, and the cultural offerings (and associated participation) have traditionally been low. The Line brings a sense of place to the areas it crosses, of belonging and cohesion to its populations.

Born in Whitechapel and raised in Barking, Akif Rahman thought for many years that the area around the River Lea was just a tangle of motorways. One day in 2021, as London was emerging from COVID lockdowns, his sister showed him an advert to be a guide on The

Catherine Sizer (above), and Akif Rahman outside the House Mill

Line. His application was successful, and he trained to engage with strangers – couples, families, the elderly. In summer, guides position themselves in pairs next to particular works and connect with passers-by. For many visitors, being shown a work of art is a moment of discovery and wonder – what someone might have assumed was scaffolding, is, when they look up, a sculpture of birds poised on poles by Tracey Emin.

Guides also bring people together – elderly people having conversations with young guides; new arrivals and longtime inhabitants; participants in group activities – and generate a sense of belonging to the area and shared pride in the works of art on display. Catherine refers to her fellow wellbeing walkers as 'The Hug Club'; its members have become friends and family to her, a group she always looks forward to seeing in the café next to Ron Haselden's *Diver*. Amar's walks, although solitary, also have a social dimension: 'Whether it's a nod to a fellow walker or a conversation sparked by a sculpture, there is a quiet understanding that this place is special. Public art creates a kind of dialogue – both with ourselves and with others.' Accessibility also brings people together: Akif remembers the impact on many Line-goers of Thomas J Price's sculpture of a young black woman looking at her mobile phone, *Reaching Out* – a work of art showing someone people could relate to.

Niyi's fellow co-commissioners, while all local, came from a broad range of backgrounds: from social housing-dweller to penthouse owner, 'people of a different tribe'. 'I would never have met these people otherwise,' Niyi reflected, and, even if he had, he would never have had the opportunity to get to know them as well as he did – he recalled his pleasure as, over the weeks, he grew to understand and enjoy the subtle sense of humour of one group member.

The Line connects 'tribes' across all age groups. In 2022, The Line organised a dance performance with related workshops which brought together English National Ballet (ENB) and Akademi (a South Asian dance group) and two local secondary schools, St Angela's Ursuline School, a Catholic girls' school, and Mulberry School for Girls, whose pupils are predominantly Muslim. Students from each gained a new understanding of dance, with participants also feeding back that they had enjoyed 'being able to find people like me' and saying how much they had 'like[d] how everyone connects in some way' across the two schools. Similarly, Associate Artists at ENB and Akademi appreciated getting to know and learning from each other.

As part of her commission, Helen Cammock spent time with local people with a view to having a changing display of locally produced works on show alongside her own piece. To facilitate this, she delivered workshops to a variety of groups. On the day we met her, she was having a session with Poplar HARCA's Knit, Natter and Craft group and had also conducted a workshop with Somali families. Thirty-six works have been produced as part of these programmes, each of which will be displayed next to the bridge for a month. When I walked The Line one cold morning in February, I was struck by a beautiful drawing in the series by Kieran Jamieson, a London College of Fashion student, with the words:

Your strength is admiring. You've fought so valiant. The battle you face will leave a trace, but those wounds are healing. Strong women emerging.

The Line has become an important resource for local schools. Zenab Bhuta is the Art Lead at Vicarage Primary School in Newham, a school with around 885 pupils with a high number of Special Educational Needs and Disability (SEND) students. She worked closely with London-based artist Rana Begum, at the time of her installation *No. 1104 Catching Colour* at London City Island, with Rana presenting at school assembly and participating in art classes. Rana used a torch to explain light and shadows to Year 3 children as they worked with coloured netting to create pieces inspired by Rana's mesh forms. Zenab then took twenty of her Year 5 pupils to see the sculpture at London City Island. They were fascinated to hear about the installation process from Rana, how long it had taken, how the work was connected to its mooring poles. It was also an opportunity for children to meet a successful artist who, as a Muslim person of South Asian heritage, came from a similar background.

Vicarage Primary School is also one of three local schools recently to have embarked on a collaborative project with The Line, *Spaces to Explore: Prioritising Process in Creative*

Zenab Bhuta in her classroom at Vicarage Primary School (above), and Gino Brignoli at Cody Dock

Learning. Zenab was particularly interested in how she could make the most of the school's additional SEND classroom and asked The Line whether an artist could help her give art classes to this particular group of pupils. Davinia-Ann Robinson was chosen and has been working with SEND children in clay as well as with drawing, helping them create their own works of art. The artist will also be talking to the school assembly and running classes involving parents as well as CPD (Continuing Professional Development) sessions with teachers from across the school. 'Davinia-Ann will be presenting to all our teachers right across the curriculum from arts to science subjects. The Line works as well for a nature-based outing as it does for an arts-focused one,' Zenab explained.

The crossover between art and nature is a constant theme of The Line. The tidal stretch of the River Lea was made accessible by members of Cody Dock, and now The Line runs through Cody Dock itself. 'The area had been a black hole in most people's mental maps of London. We opened the path, but it was The Line that put it on the map more broadly, with the tidal Lea suddenly becoming a destination when the sculpture trail was opened', said Simon Myers, Cody Dock's founder. 'There has been a natural collaboration between Cody Dock and The Line,' said Gino Brignoli, Biodiversity Officer at Cody Dock. 'Our longest-serving volunteer found us from being a regular Line-walker.'

The relationship between The Line and Cody Dock is correlative: The Line's artistic starting point complements Cody Dock's ecological emphasis. When you walk The Line to look at the sculptures, you cannot help noticing the plants and wildlife all around, and a number of The Line's programmes, such as the Wellbeing Walks, are focused on the natural qualities of the walk. 'The sculptures and artistic interventions make people slow down,' said Gino. Similarly, participants and volunteers in Cody Dock's bird walks and other activities frequently stop to discuss The Line's artworks. The ecology of this part of the River Lea is all about how nature has dealt with the post-industrial brownfield habitat – The Line's artistic interventions represent a human reaction to that habitat.

Nadia Kerbouche, the genial owner of the café at Cody Dock, regularly walks The Line and has many Line-goers among her customers. For her, Cody Dock and The Line are indissociable, a joyful package of art and nature: 'Cody Dock is part of my life, I love the river, I love The Line, I love art.'

The siting of the pieces on The Line also creates opportunities for this cross-over between art and nature. The sandblasted York stones of Simon Faithfull's *Journey Across Europe and Africa* lie nestled in the grass framed by daisies or wild orchids depending on the time of year, perhaps also providing shelter for arty earthworms beneath. Cormorants perch atop Helen Cammock's installation, as if drawn to its text about the tides below. Gino recalled how early one morning he saw a fox crossing the river using the Madge Gill bridge.

The Line's relationship with the House Mill, at the top of the tidal Lea, is also symbiotic. Here The Line's contemporary art and wellbeing programmes meet the magnificent eighteenth-century architecture and industrial history of the House Mill, the world's largest surviving tidal mill. The House Mill hosts two of The Line's pieces, an untitled work by Madge Gill and a sculpture by Virginia Overton, *Untitled (Juniper)*. Both are integrated into the architecture of the mill, with Virginia's golden weathervane forming a pendant to the historic one on the Clock Mill opposite. Participants in The Line's Wellbeing Walks are always given a warm welcome by Beverley Charters, who runs the House Mill, as they stop at the café. Beverley's knowledge of the history of the mill, generously shared with visitors and passers-by, brings this setting to life.

Simon Myers at Cody Dock (left), and Nadia Kerbouche at her café at Cody Dock

Beverley Charters at the House Mill (above), and Megan Piper at Three Mills

Many people I spoke to clearly regard The Line as home or an extension of it. For Amar, who lives 100 yards away, The Line is his (and his dog Pepe's) magical back garden in which he has been able to develop his artistic and nature-based interests – he volunteers for a local swan feeding project – but which has also assumed a spiritual and therapeutic dimension. For Catherine, who was brought up nearby but had lost touch with the area, The Line represents a form of homecoming, with the added comfort of seeing the offices of Phaidon, the publisher with whom she had worked while at London College of Fashion, on her walks along the river. Niyi is proud to have helped improve his neighbourhood.

The Line also evokes a sense of more distant homes: for local children of West African heritage, taking part in a class with Ghanaian artist Serge Attukwei Clottey, in which they connected online with children in Accra and participated in a procession, gave them a strong sense of pride and belonging.

The sense of local engagement and pride is felt particularly strongly when a temporary installation is removed. Megan Piper, the visionary co-founder of The Line, described how individual works become 'part of people's everyday lives'. 'For several years we showed Joanna Rajkowska's *The Hatchling*, a giant blackbird's egg placed on the ground near Cody Dock. People were encouraged to hug the egg, press their ears to it to hear the sounds of hatching chicks inside. For months after we had deinstalled the piece, people would ask where it had gone.'

Amar has taken to feeding the pigeons on the spot where Tracey Emin's *A Moment Without You* stood for several years. For him, the temporary and rotating nature of the art on The Line ties into his Buddhist faith: 'I see the end of this sculpture in this place as a sign of impermanence, just like nature.'

Or, as Megan put it: 'The Line will never be finished. It is in its nature to be dynamic, living.'

MERIDIAN LINES AND SANKOFA TIME

EMMA DABIRI

On a bitterly cold but beautiful winter day, with the sun finally making a glorious entrance after months that felt like years of absence, I travelled to North Greenwich station to visit The Line for the first time.

The trip signalled my first encounter with an electric bike, too, and honestly, whizzing along the cycle path, following the bends of the river, studded with so many arresting, thought-provoking works of art – the various sculptures and installations that constitute The Line's 'collection' – is an incredible way to spend an afternoon. As a former long-term resident of East London, the experience was made all the more memorable by the sense of familiarity unmoored. As I followed The Line's lines of flight, which deviated just slightly from some of the well-worn tracks I once walked, I discovered universes previously unknown to me in places I had lived in close proximity to for many years.

With the sunlight diffused through the wispy fronds of an ancient reed bed and glinting off the surface of the Thames as well as the mirrored glass vestiges to capital – the offices of HSBC, Barclays and Citibank that hug the bank of the river – I soared down the pathway to *Tribe and Tribulation*, a wooden sculpture designed by Ghanaian artist Serge Attukwei Clottey. *Tribe and Tribulation* was the first commission of *Longitudinal Dialogues: Cultural Conversations on the Meridian*, a project that considers The Line's location on the Greenwich Meridian in London as a starting point for global cultural exchange.

Serge Attukwei Clottey's *Tribe and Tribulation* at Greenwich Peninsula

This is, of course, a global cultural exchange of historically unjust and wildly unequal distributions of power. The establishment of the Greenwich Meridian, which organised the world into the time zones it operates according to to this day, situated the UK, and Greenwich specifically, at the centre of time! This was part of a global colonial project, where time itself was colonised and transformed into a commodity – the invention of a world in which time is money, and money is time. It is the organising principle of an economic system that demanded the transformation of African people and their descendants into categories of the subhuman. Men, women and children, reclassified as 'slaves', comprised the labour force required to maximise profit for the plantation economies that would go on to finance the establishment of West India Docks, which *Tribe and Tribulation* confronts across the Thames all these centuries later. Clottey repurposes older materials; a common characteristic of African and African diasporic art practices, providing a dramatic point of contrast to the metal, glass and concrete behemoths it stands in (not) silent watch of, across the water. The materials used include painted timber from Ghanaian fishing boats, demonstrating sustainability in practice – especially pertinent in this time of ecological crises that have been brought about by the same extractive economic system that sought dominion over Africans, Indigenous peoples and the very land itself.

In 1884, a team of international delegates – white European men, unsurprisingly – met at a conference in Washington, DC, and decided that Greenwich would be the prime meridian of the new global time zone system – the centre of world time and navigation. With nearly two-thirds of the world's ships already using charts based on the Greenwich Meridian, this location was chosen because it offered the least disruption, facilitating an easier transition to a single prime meridian. The UK had already determined the logic of the maritime technologies of capitalism. It just now became official. It is little coincidence that this was the very same year the Berlin Conference, or 'the Scramble for Africa', took place – the event where Belgium, France, Germany, the United Kingdom, Italy, Portugal and Spain annexed Africa among themselves. This facilitated the invasion, conquest and colonisation of the continent to begin in earnest, replacing the previous economic model which had favoured the kidnapping and enslavement of millions of Africans to toil on the plantations of the New World. The Scramble for Africa created the borders of the Gold Coast, the nation that would eventually become Ghana. The prime meridian runs from Greenwich to Ghana, and continues to organise time in a country whose very borders it also imagined.

Standing over five metres tall, the totemic structure *Tribe and Tribulation* also contains a sound installation with recordings from Cape Coast Castle, Elmina Castle, James Fort and a location on the Meridian line in Tema, a town in south-eastern Ghana, situated on the Atlantic coast. The first three sites are former slave forts that have been designated World Heritage Sites, honouring the memories of the millions of enslaved captives who were once detained there. The sound recordings – projected to the north, south, east and west – invite the listener to consider how life at these historic sites has changed over the years, with the waters now used for fishing rather than for the trade in human life. On the day I visited *Tribe and Tribulation*, the layering of time, space and cultural memory was acutely palpable, enhanced by the presence of two white Englishmen fishing in the river in front of the sculpture, their rap music blending with the voices and aquatic sounds of the installation. When we [Megan Piper and I] spoke to them, one of them mentioned being unemployed, but described an interview he was excited about. However, until he got that job – which he seemed hopeful of – he was out here, spending his day fishing. The synchronicity between the activities taking place at both ends of the Greenwich Meridian offered a reminder of what people share on either coast, as well as what divides them.

Larry Achiampong recording for *Sanko-time*

Continuing further along the route, Larry Achiampong's audio work, *Sanko-time*, accompanies the cable car travelling between Greenwich Peninsula and the Royal Docks. Looking down, you are confronted by an awe-inspiring vision, rendered all the more majestic by the dazzlingly bright, laser-like winter sunshine illuminating the city below on this particular February afternoon. Achiampong's audio is the perfect accompaniment to the visual as he narrates a brief history, highlighting the paradox that exists in what lies beneath.

'These Royal Docks were previously a celebrated global centre for innovation and industry but for many they still represent the sting of colonialism. These docks were the birthplace of Tate and Lyle's first sugar cube ... Bank of England, British Museum ... across this island nation, many firms and fortunes were built or benefitted on the foundations of slavery in the seventeenth and eighteenth centuries ... Ramifications of the spread of Empire are still being negotiated by many of the African Caribbean Diaspora today.'

The audio then shifts into mysterious, somewhat sinister electronic music, conjuring images of a dystopian future, or perhaps present, before segueing into West African drumming and song. The name of the piece itself, *Sanko-time*, is rich with meaning. Referring to the Ghanaian concept of *Sankofa*, a Twi word from the Akan people, *Sankofa* is a metaphysical principle that highlights the necessity of taking things from the past in order to design the future that we want to create. *San* means 'to return', and the symbols that express *Sankofa* – either a bird looking backwards with its feet facing forwards or a stylised entwined heart – speak to precolonial African understandings of time as cyclical, devoid of discrete boundaries between the past, the present and the future. These are time zones determined by season and spirituality rather than economic extraction, where the ancestors, the living and unborn exist in unfolding relation to each other. It is a very different orientation to how time has been conceived in the West (and then forcibly imposed across the globe), where time is understood as linear, chronological and sequential, and since the birth of capitalism, increasingly measured in units designed to maximise profit.

Given that the meridian lines themselves are imaginary, albeit enshrined by force, violence and military power, Achiampong's creative intervention here, at the point of their origin, is a bold assertion of Black imaginary practice, just as plausible a birthplace as the European imagination and the subsequent logics they have forcibly imposed on a world designed in their own image, posing the question, why can't Black imaginary practice legitimise reality too?

Exiting the cable car, the next work I encountered was *Bird Boy*. Laura Ford's statue is so startling, perhaps counterintuitively because it's so inobtrusive. As Ford says, 'I think that a lot of sculptures stand around in quite a sort of entitled way. And I just wanted to explore whether you could make a sculpture that had uncertainty in the space, and what that did, how that activated the space.' Exuding a quietly powerful force, it's very easy to get lost standing and staring at the slight, odd, melancholy figure, youthful yet also ancient and mythic seeming, looking out across the open water towards the sleek glass modernity of City Hall – the Mayor of London's offices – beneath the cable cars which crisscross the sky overhead.

As soon as I saw *Bird Boy* I was reminded of the Spanish film *The Orphanage*. Although I watched it when it was made, almost twenty years ago, I can recall its atmosphere to this day, simultaneously heartbreaking and terrifying as it is. In the eponymous orphanage, the children who once lived there continued their search for a caregiver for many years after their deaths. One of the ghosts, a little boy who wears a sack over his head to hide a deformity as he did in life, reminded me of *Bird Boy* in particular. In his *Guardian* review of *The Orphanage*, Peter Bradshaw wrote: '[It] revives the genre's great theme: our profound yet unacknowledged fear of children. We are afraid of their vulnerability, which is our vulnerability, and the mysterious otherness of their private, mental worlds'.[1] And that is perhaps something of the power of *Bird Boy*, especially in the context it exists in. Encountering this vulnerable child, having just travelled across the river listening to Achiampong's soundscape, the history of suffering reverberates in one's mind and it's hard not to think of *Bird Boy* in the context of migrant children, refugee children, separated children, or even enslaved children. It is extremely affecting.

Continuing the route north, with *On WindTides*, Helen Cammock expresses her concern with the ways in which collective knowledge is built through historical narrative, and examines how these narratives are intimately connected to structures of power. Comprising large-scale text on the sides of a sixty-metre cable bridge over the River Lea just north of Cody Dock, the first text of *On WindTides* reads, 'we fold ourselves across the tides', the second, 'from silt to land sometimes we live as wind blown sand'.

This work is inspired by the site of the bridge itself, which straddles the River Lea, connecting Tower Hamlets and Newham. As Cammock explains, these boroughs comprise a rich tapestry, made up of the stories of people from 'many different histories, cultures, and experiences. Some people are newer residents than others, but each has a different story of why they settle here, and the river running through carrying winds and tides from other parts of the world.' As a woman who moved to London from Dublin in my teens, this notion resonates deeply, but even long before I left home, I was already the product of colonial migrations. My Nigerian grandparents came to Scotland and then Dublin in the late 1940s to study, and while they returned to Nigeria in the 1950s, my father would move back to Ireland in the 1970s, where

Laura Ford's *Bird Boy (without a tail)* in the Royal Docks

he met my mother. My mother, a white Irish woman, was, however, born in the Caribbean and spent her childhood in Tobago, because her father – also an Irishman – worked for the British colonial administration in Trinidad and Tobago, a civil engineer who designed much of the island's roads, bridges and transport infrastructure. The tentacles of the British Empire had dispersed my family all over the world long before these migrations resulted in my birth, and I in turn migrated to the imperial centre. These movements speak profoundly to Cammock's interest 'in the intersections between individual lived experience and histories', or to repeat Achiampong's words, the 'ramifications of the spread of Empire still being negotiated'.

Perhaps one of my favourite pieces, however, is Cammock's short film *The Lay Shaft Drive is Down*, which was commissioned by The Line in 2023, filmed on location at the beautiful House Mill in Bromley-by-Bow, whose original tidal mills date back to the Domesday Book of 1056 (the current mill was built in 1776). In Cammock's elegiac film, the artist sings rounds of folk songs which are interwoven with a spoken word performance. She connects the intimately interwoven relationship between English factory workers during the Industrial Revolution and the enslaved Black people forced to toil in the unremitting labour of the plantation. The fetishisation of productivity under capitalism and the way it overworks but eventually underutilises the labourer, whom it then disregards – a theme Cammock explores in the performance – seemed to reverberate through the centuries, echoing in the fate of the unemployed fisherman we had encountered earlier on The Line.

In thinking about identities and how we might imagine them beyond ethnicity, race, religion or nation, and the role that rivers could play in creating less exclusionary, more communal kinships, Professor Tao Leigh Goffe shared an exchange she had with a mountain tour guide in Tahiti. He asked her what river she was born closest to, as well as which river she drank from every day, explaining that in Tahiti, 'the answers to these two questions say more about a person than their name ever could'.[2] Goffe suggests that to define relation in this way, according to a 'hydrological orientation', is to place ourselves in climate history. That it is also inclined towards a 'less individualistic and exceptionalist, and of more of a collective spirit of being'. Members of the Dark Lab (a collective research group founded by Goffe) come together to imagine how the violent architecture of sugarcane refineries, mills and old plantations could possibly be repurposed for anti-capitalist scientific aims,[3] a proposal that certainly felt pertinent here in the context of Three Mills.

Film still from Helen Cammock's *The Lay Shaft Drive is Down*

Back at Greenwich, another of my favourite pieces is Antony Gormley's *Quantum Cloud*, a sculpture of galvanised steel. Foregrounding the viewer's influence on the viewed – a feature of both quantum physics and art – *Quantum Cloud* was inspired by conversations between Gormley and quantum physicist Basil Hiley. Gormley explains that he was interested in considering the fundamental question: How do we relate to space, time and the elements? This is a question of how matter and meaning constitute each other, not unlike Cammock's interest in the 'intersections between individual lived experiences and histories'. Moreover, we might also consider it in relation to advances in quantum research that have shown that time operates in a non-linear, non-chronological fashion, and how that corresponds to the cyclical or co-existing understanding of time in African metaphysics.

How much time do we humans have left on this planet if we don't reimagine our relationship to it, if we refuse to transition from the pursuit of profit at the cost of human and non-human life, and if we refuse to deviate from the thinking that created the system so many of these artworks challenge? The afternoon gave me much to reflect on, not only how acts of imagination can be used to ask these questions, but to inspire solutions.

1 Peter Bradshaw, *The Guardian*, 21 March 2008
2 *Dark Laboratory*, Tao Leigh Goffe, Hamish Hamilton, 2025: 70
3 *Dark Laboratory*, Tao Leigh Goffe, Hamish Hamilton, 2025: 71

THE LINE

Youth Guide
Supervisor
Youth Guide
Supervisor
citi

HSBC
BARCLAYS
STATE STREET
Ask me about art on The Line

ALEX CHINNECK

***A Bullet from a Shooting Star*, 2015**
Galvanised steel
Height 35 m
September 2015–July 2025

Commissioned by Greenwich Peninsula

A Bullet from a Shooting Star is an upside-down electricity pylon balancing on its tip and leaning at a precarious angle, as though shot to earth from the sky. Greenwich Peninsula was once home to the largest gasworks in Europe and the pylon evokes this industrial history. The latticed steelwork reflects the visual and material language of multiple structures on the peninsula, particularly the (former) neighbouring gas holder and the tilting structural elements of the Millennium Dome (The O2). Chinneck says his work seeks to make 'the everyday world feel momentarily extraordinary'.

HSBC
BARCLAYS

THOMSON & CRAIGHEAD

***Here*, 2013**
Custom signpost
264 × 82 × 12 cm
May 2015–ongoing

Here is a standard UK road sign pointing north and reading, 'Here 24,859'. The installation marks the distance from the sign around the circumference of the earth. Craighead said, 'We're trying to get people to imagine that if they set off walking, that they would eventually reappear at the same point.' The current placement of the sculpture on the Greenwich Meridian is particularly relevant, which is located at 0° longitude.

citi
HSBC

RICHARD WILSON

A Slice of Reality, 2000
Sliced vertical section of a sand dredger
21.3 × 10.6 × 8.8 m
2000–ongoing

Commissioned by The New Millennium Experience Company

Standing permanently on the foreshore of the Thames, this sculpture is a one-eighth slice of what was originally the Arco Trent, an ocean-going sand dredger. The artist, who is known for his playful architectural interventions, acquired the Arco Trent and cut a vertical section of the ship, intentionally exposing the living quarters and engine room to viewers and the elements. Wilson describes the work as a 'sound bite', communicating Greenwich's rich maritime history, while referencing the manner in which the prime meridian slices through the peninsula.

WARNING
ZW

ZW
WILSON

citi
HSBC
BARCLAYS

SERGE ATTUKWEI CLOTTEY

Tribe and Tribulation, 2022
Co-curated with Arup Phase 2
Mixed media and audio equipment
550 × 140 × 140 cm
July 2022–ongoing

Serge Attukwei Clottey's totemic sculpture stands at over five metres tall and comprises four stacked cubes that are made of reclaimed wood, including painted timber from Ghanaian fishing boats. An embedded sound installation features recordings from three former slave forts and a location on the Greenwich Meridian in Tema, Ghana. The recordings invite the listener to consider how life at these historic sites has changed, with the waters now used by local fishermen. The work was developed through the artist's research residency at Royal Museums Greenwich and reflects his interest in our relationship to the ocean, migration and the afterlife of objects.

Tribe and Tribulation was the first project in The Line's *Longitudinal Dialogues* programme, which takes its location on the Greenwich Meridian as a starting point for global cultural exchange. As part of the engagement programme for this commission – working in collaboration with Foundation for Contemporary Art, Ghana – workshops were held that connected six primary schools in London and Accra. Around 600 children participated in artist-led sessions, using recyclable materials to create masks inspired by Clottey's practice. On 26 May 2022, at the same time in both cities, the children took part in a procession to celebrate the project (see page 64).

THAMES PATH
GREENWICH
IN EMERGENCY
RING
ASK FOR COASTGUARD
QUOTE SITE REF.
GR60

HSBC
BARCLAYS

KP

FOO

LBS
THE MADISON

GARY HUME

Liberty Grip, 2008
Patinated and painted bronze and railway sleepers
553 x 297 x 190 cm
May 2015–ongoing

Liberty Grip is a bronze sculpture composed of three sections, each modelled on the arm of a shop mannequin. The sculpture blurs the line between figuration and abstraction, while its scale and material allude to traditional commemorative statuary. According to the artist, the playful, candy-pink tip of each limb signifies flesh and humanises the work. He says, 'Liberty Grip [is] a cheerleading hold and this was made during the [Iraq] War ... I was really intrigued and perplexed by American power, and how they celebrate it, and part of that celebration is through cheerleading.'

CITY ISLAND
Uber Boat
Uber Boat

ANTONY GORMLEY

Quantum Cloud, 2000
Galvanised steel
29 × 16 × 10 m
2000–ongoing

Commissioned by The New Millennium Experience Company

Antony Gormley's *Quantum Cloud* comprises over 3,500 interconnected steel tetrahedrons radiating from a central figure, which, like many of Gormley's works, is based on his own body. The twenty-nine-metre structure was inspired by conversations between Gormley and the quantum physicist Basil Hiley. Evoking the quantum age, it suggests an unstable relation between energy and mass and questions whether the body is produced by the field or the field by the body. Gormley said, 'I've called it *Quantum Cloud* because I'm very aware that the truth about reality is not in appearance, it's to do with energy, and actually everything is in flux and everything is becoming, everything is in a form of transformation.'

Uber Boat

Do business
in the cloud
FAST

STERLING RUBY

***Consolidator #654321*, 2009**
Aluminium
175 × 234 × 643 cm
May 2015–August 2019

Consolidator #654321 is a large aluminium sculpture that references traditional cannon monuments, often used to commemorate the location of a historical fortification or battleground. The shape of this work also resembles a coffin, evoking the power implied in political monuments, while at the same time pointing to an inherent powerlessness within those structures. The sculpture belongs to a series of the artist's geometric works made in many different materials, including wood, Formica, steel and bronze. The number in its title references the hexadecimal code for the colour.

Crystal

MARTIN CREED

***Work No.700*, 2007**
Steel beams
145 × 29 × 1,200 cm
May 2015–December 2016

Work No.700 is composed of three progressively slimmer steel I-beams that are balanced on top of each other. These beams, each twelve metres in length, were created for use in bridge or building construction. By neatly stacking them, Creed has replaced their functionality with a focus on form and, in turn, has created a work of simple, unexpected beauty. This sculpture is the largest work from Creed's 'stack' series, in which the artist stacks everyday objects, from chairs to plant pots. Creed said, 'I think of a lot of my art as a simple frame through which people can see all the chaos of the world.'

CROWNE PLAZA

EDUARDO PAOLOZZI

Vulcan, 1999
Bronze
800 × 300 × 300 cm
May 2015–June 2017

Vulcan, after whom this sculpture is named, was the Roman god of fire and metalworking. He forged weapons for the gods and is shown in Paolozzi's sculpture brandishing the blacksmith's hammer. Influenced by Surrealism, early modernism and Cubism, the figure is depicted as half man and half machine – a possible commentary on the sometimes gruelling work of a sculptor. *Vulcan* was one of the artist's last works.

JAMES BALMFORTH

Inhibition Point, 2015
Cor-Ten and stainless steel
300 × 39 × 39 cm
April 2016–January 2017

Inhibition Point is a three-metre-tall Cor-Ten steel column with its central section gouged out, leaving just enough of the steel to prevent the sculpture from collapsing. The work confronts the viewer with the realities of force, gravity, balance and duration. Both the scale and implied weight of the sculpture heighten the power of the viewer's experience. *Inhibition Point* was created specifically for the Royal Docks.

Take two
in the cloud
IFS

LAURA FORD

***Bird Boy (without a tail)*, 2011**
Bronze
115 × 50 × 45 cm
March 2020–ongoing

Laura Ford's sculptures present a complex interplay between vulnerability and menace. She uses humour and an acute observation of the human condition to engage with wider social and political issues. *Bird Boy* is a figure of a lost child wearing a bird costume. Standing motionless on a pontoon in the Royal Docks, *Bird Boy* seems to hope he will go unnoticed but, despite his scale, his presence is powerful and commands attention. Ford said, 'A lot of sculptures stand around in quite an entitled way, and I wanted to explore whether you could make a sculpture that had [a sense of] uncertainty in the space, and what that did, how that activated the space.'

CITY HALL

MADGE GILL

Nature in Mind
Co-curated with Sophie Dutton

Nature in Mind was an exhibition across five sites in Newham that celebrated the inspiration Madge Gill found in nature. It featured large-scale installations – the majority of which are still in situ – that reflect her process of bringing her largest works outside, into the garden, to see them in their entirety. She once stated, 'If I were a man, I would have gone abroad and studied botany.' Gill was a self-taught artist who lived in Newham for over forty years. The reproductions on display were drawn from London Borough of Newham Heritage Service's collection of over 1,200 works by the artist, which were donated to the council by her family when she died in 1961.

Untitled (x6), c. 1930–54
Original works: Ink and watercolour on card, 50 x 61.5 cm
Reproductions: Dibond, 240 x 229 cm
June 2021–June 2025

Gill created her works on whatever she could find, from postcards to large-scale calico. These six works include her signature black and white drawings and also highlight her unreserved use of vibrant colour. Located within an avenue of trees, the installation reflected the surrounding nature and the energy of the environment in which they existed.

LARRY ACHIAMPONG

***What I Hear I Keep*, 2022**
Spun polyester and cotton cambric flag
120 x 180 cm
June 2022–April 2024

Original design commissioned by De La Warr Pavilion

What I Hear I Keep is one of a number of Pan-African flags created by the artist. It features green, black and red to reflect the land, the people and the struggles the continent has endured, and yellow-gold to represent a new day and prosperity. The formation of fifty-four stars represents each of the countries on the African continent, while the chevron shapes allude to the act of sending and receiving messages that resonate. Installed on the roof of the Good Hotel in the Royal Docks, the work is also the graphic used in signage for Achiampong's *Sanko-time*, The Line's first sound commission.

HSBC
BARCLAYS

***Sanko-time*, 2020**
Audio work, accessible through The Line's website
Two parts, each 10 minutes
2020–ongoing

Sanko-time is a site-specific audio work that was created by the artist to accompany the twenty-minute round-trip over the River Thames on the London Cable Car. Threaded with a powerful narrative about the legacy of colonialism, *Sanko-time* is a hypnotic synthesis of oral histories from London Museum's sound collection, audio recordings by local primary school children, field recordings from London and Accra, and music. The work reflects on the indelibility of the British Empire on the areas that are local to The Line. *Sanko-time* is a concept developed by the artist that relates to the Ghanaian Twi word *Sankofa*, which roughly translates as 'to go back for what has been left behind' and alludes to using the past to prepare for the future.

GOOD HOTEL
the living room
bar & terrace
ibis

LONDON
LOVE

YINKA ILORI

***Types of Happiness*, 2019**
Mild stainless steel frame covered with glass fibre and resin
320 × 122 × 144 cm each
June 2023–ongoing

Types of Happiness comprises two ten-foot-tall sculptural chairs, brightly coloured with a Dutch wax print-like pattern. They are part of a collection of six chairs through which the artist explores sixteen different types of happiness, including pride, strength, excitement, calmness, and determination. Each of the chairs uses the same colours in different combinations meant to evoke different kinds of happiness. Ilori said, 'Each chair has its own feeling, strength, like unity, power … the whole idea is to get people thinking about how we look at colour and how colour makes us feel.' The two chairs on The Line represent happiness and pride.

CROWNE PLAZA
ibis
NOVOTEL

MADGE GILL

***Red Women*, 1949**
Original work: Pencil and ink on paper, 75 × 900 cm
Reproduction: Dibond, 75 × 900 cm
June 2021–ongoing

As well as meticulous small-scale postcards, Gill created monumental works, skilfully exploring different techniques and formats, including paints, inks and textiles. *Red Women* was created in a single evening. On the reverse of the original drawing, she wrote 'May 19 – 49. Evening 8pm'. Working along a roll of paper, the artist would not have been able to see the drawing in full while making it. This is the only work in the exhibition that has been reproduced at its original size. Due to its scale, this nine-metre-long work had never been displayed in its entirety.

KATIE SCHWAB

***a cloud + a fence*, 2024**
Vitreous enamel and powder-coated aluminium, sign fixings, powder-coated steel rail, paint
Various sizes along a 570 m trail
July 2024–ongoing

a cloud + a fence is a series of blue enamel shapes and painted street furniture. It marks the journey between Star Lane DLR station and Cody Dock and is a collaboration between the artist and local residents, supported by Newham Council. Emerging from a series of workshops with local people, the installation references the area's cultural, natural and industrial heritage. The vibrant blue echoes synthetic dyes like Meldola's Blue, which was invented locally, and natural dyes like blue indigo, which were used by textile producers all along the Lower Lea throughout the eighteenth and nineteenth centuries.

P
Mon - Sat
8 am - 6.30 pm
Permit holders ICT
or
Pay by phone
020 7005 0055
quoting location
800338
Max stay 4 hours
no return
within 1 hour

DANGER OF DEATH

11a South Crescent
pulse
Canning Town Depot

HSBC
HSBC
CODY DOCK
CAFE OPEN

DAMIEN HIRST

Sensation, **2003**
Painted bronze
198 × 318 × 165 cm
May 2015–November 2019

Sensation is a painted bronze sculpture that is based on a highly coloured anatomical model of a 3 mm cross-section of human skin. As the bronze has been painted and the model of human skin has been enlarged to a monumental scale, the sculpture challenges art historical and scientific traditions and conventions. By revealing the details of the body's largest organ, the sculpture draws attention to things that are often overlooked, exploring the complex relationship between scientific fact and the mysterious realities of life.

JOANNA RAJKOWSKA

The Hatchling, 2019
Acrylic plaster, sound equipment, paint
180 × 240 × 180 cm
November 2019–February 2022

The Hatchling is a large-scale replica of the egg of a blackbird, one of Britain's most common birds, known for its melodious song and distinctive blue-green speckled eggs. The whole egg acts as a speaker, inviting visitors to touch and listen carefully to recordings of new, fragile hatchlings. In winter, British blackbirds are joined by large numbers of migrants from Europe, mainly Scandinavia, the Baltic States, Russia and Germany. The sculpture reminds us of the many birds that live with us in cities, and of the fragility of the natural environment – the survival of which determines our own existence.

MADGE GILL

Star Lane · Cody Dock

Untitled, c. 1930–54
Original work: Ink on card, 50 × 61 cm
Reproduction: PVC banner, 7.8 × 62 m
June 2021–ongoing

This sixty-metre-long installation over the River Lea is a section of a drawing that highlights Gill's use of free-flowing abstract forms, flowers and petals, reflecting her fascination with the natural world. Her confident use of colour imbues the work with life, transforming a utilitarian cable bridge and framing the ever-changing landscape beyond.

Madge Gill
Nature in Mind

HELEN CAMMOCK

On WindTides, **2024**
Bridge: stencil cut powder-coated steel letters
Cabinet: powder-coated steel and concrete ballast
Bridge: 1.8 × 60 m
Cabinet: 1.9 × 1.2 m
May 2024–ongoing

Spanning the River Lea, *On WindTides* is a large-scale text installation that explores movement, migration and change. It consists of short prose on either side of a sixty-metre-long cable bridge that connects Newham and Tower Hamlets, just north of Cody Dock. One side of the bridge reads, 'we fold ourselves across the tides', while the other side reads, 'from silt to land sometimes we live as wind blown sand'. The letters sit proud of the bridge, creating shadows with the movement of the sun. Supported by Newham Council, this work was co-commissioned with local residents and includes an exhibition cabinet featuring a changing display of text-based works on paper, created by members of the local community during workshops led by the artist.

we fold ourselves acro

the
tides

from silt to land somet

s we live as wind blown sand

HSBC

ABIGAIL FALLIS

***DNA DL90*, 2003**
Trolleys and steel
939 × 300 × 300 cm
May 2015–ongoing

DNA DL90 is a sculpture composed of twenty-two shopping trolleys arranged in the shape of a double helix. The work was commissioned by a supermarket chain to mark the fiftieth anniversary of American biologist James Watson and English physicist Francis Crick's discovery of DNA's double-helix structure, which was based on Rosalind Franklin's X-ray diffraction images of DNA. Their findings were fundamental to the understanding of muscular dystrophy. The commission served to raise awareness of the disease and, according to Fallis, the trolleys are a symbol of modern society's culture of consumerism, which she believes has become part of our genetic make-up.

wind blows sand

SIMON FAITHFULL

0°00 Navigation Part II: A Journey Across Europe and Africa, 2023
Co-curated with Arup Phase 2
Sandblasted York stones
Total length 30 m
September 2023–ongoing

This installation is part of Simon Faithfull's *0°00 Navigation* series, exploring the paradoxes and absurdities of the Greenwich Meridian. The work features drawings that have been sandblasted into thirty-eight York paving slabs and set along the River Lea towpath. The drawings capture scenes from Faithfull's journey tracing the 0° line through France, Spain, Algeria, Burkina Faso, Togo and Ghana. This exploration of the Greenwich Meridian is the second iteration of The Line's *Longitudinal Dialogues* programme. Faithfull says, 'The piece does something that quite a few of my works do, which is to transport the viewer from their local situation and extrapolate out conceptually to a planetary scale.'

EVA ROTHSCHILD

***Living Spring*, 2011**
Painted steel
413 × 90 × 40 cm
August 2021–ongoing

Living Spring is a slender, four-metre-tall sculpture composed of metal tubes striped in black, red and green. Situated at the end of a line of mature trees, its form resembles a sapling. This is one of a number of branch-like sculptures the artist has made. She explains that the first was inspired by the most basic idea of making a sculpture, thinking about the Stone Age and the idea of a painted twig or rock – something that you separate from the natural world and name as a work of art, rather than a tool or something else you find lying around. Its reference to nature contrasts with Rothschild's highly controlled use of colour. She is interested in the way we give meaning and symbolism to inanimate things and has described her work as 'Magic Minimalism'.

Generously donated to The Line by The Christian Levett Collection and FAMM (Femmes Artistes du Musée de Mougins)

VILNIUS RIOT SQUAD

TRACEY EMIN

A Moment Without You, 2017
Bronze and patinated steel
Dimensions variable
July 2021–November 2024

Tracey Emin's *A Moment Without You* comprises five sculpted bronze birds positioned on top of a series of four-metre-tall poles. For Emin, the diminutive life-sized forms serve as symbols of hope, faith and spirituality: 'I've always had the idea that birds are angels of this earth and that they represent freedom.' Emin has commented that 'most public sculptures are a symbol of power which I find oppressive and dark … I wanted something that had a magic and an alchemy, something which would appear and disappear and not dominate.' With a backdrop of Three Mills, these small creatures benignly watched the world below and created space for reflection.

3

VIRGINIA OVERTON

Untitled (Juniper), 2014
Mild steel, gold leaf and paint
288 × 106 × 113 cm
July 2021–ongoing

Untitled (Juniper) is a fully functioning weathervane, decorated with a gilded juniper tree that catches and reflects the light as it tracks the direction of the wind. Overton's work is similar to the traditional weathervanes that are still visible across London, including on the roof of the nearby Clock Mill. Its ornamental feature, the juniper tree, is common to Tennessee, where Overton grew up. Juniper berries have long been used to flavour gin, so the work speaks to its location at Three Mills, which was the site of a gin distillery until 1941.

S
N

BILL VIOLA

Three Women, 2008
Colour high-definition video on flat panel display mounted vertically on wall
155.5 x 92.5 x 12.7 cm
9:06 minutes
Performers: Anika, Cornelia and Helena Ballent

Transfiguration, 2007 (below, left)
Black-and-white high-definition video on flat panel display mounted vertically on wall; stereo sound with subwoofer (2.1)
155.5 x 92.5 x 12.7 cm
7:00 minutes
Performer: Blake Viola

Howard, 2008 (below, right)
Colour high-definition video on flat panel display mounted vertically on wall
63 x 35.5 x 6 cm
11:31 minutes
Performer: Howard Ferguson

May–August 2015

Three videos from Bill Viola's *Transfigurations* series were presented at the House Mill, a Grade I listed eighteenth-century tidal mill. In the videos, apparitions slowly emerge from complete darkness and move towards the viewer. As we begin to decipher their shapes, they move through an imperceptible wall of water, passing from obscurity to clarity, from death to life, and back again. Viola captures the figures contemplating their journey between two realms, and in the process urges us to confront significant questions about our existence through subtle metamorphoses.

TRIBUTARIES

July–September 2023

Tributaries was an exhibition that featured five artist films responding to human relationships with bodies of water. Situated in the House Mill, it brought together work by Martha Atienza, Ursula Biemann, Hanna Ljungh, Daniela Medina Poch & Elizabeth Gallón Droste and Alberta Whittle. The exhibition explored the theme of water through global histories and geographies of trade, colonial legacies and the climate crisis.

The House Mill is the world's largest surviving tidal mill and is increasingly vulnerable to flooding. In both subject matter and context, the exhibition explored the myriad ways we live with water.

Alberta Whittle
***between a whisper and a cry*, 2019**
Installation view
HD film, 41 minutes

MARTHA ATIENZA

***How to Civilize a Waterfall*, 2010**
4-minute video

In *How to Civilize a Waterfall*, the artist performs an authoritative confrontation with a waterfall, as she tries to persuade it to turn into a hydroelectric power plant. The work reveals humanity's comical and paradoxical relationship with nature. The encounter becomes an emotional and almost spiritual experience. Wildly shouting and gesticulating, the artist unsuccessfully tries to convince a waterfall of the advantages of replacing it with a dam.

DANIELA MEDINA POCH & ELIZABETH GALLÓN DROSTE

***Intersecting Mediterranean(s) from the Perspective of its Regional Rivers*, 2021–23**
8-minute video

Intersecting Mediterranean(s) from the Perspective of its Regional Rivers is a collaborative research project and film that addresses hidden histories along the Mediterranean. Medina Poch and Droste explore the area as a complex and living archive of myths, memories, relationships and cultural connections. Through intersecting voices from the Po, Isonzo/Soča, Neretva, Cem Cijevna, Düden, Kishon, Nile, Medjerda, Chelif, Moulouya, Ebro and the Rhône rivers, the film looks at how the freshwater rivers that flow into the Mediterranean Sea carry voices and histories that challenge a Eurocentric view. *Intersecting Mediterranean(s) from the Perspective of its Regional Rivers* hopes to acknowledge the specificities of the region and invites viewers to reconsider its past, present and future.

***between a whisper and a cry*, 2019**
HD film, 41 minutes

between a whisper and a cry is a multi-layered film that links together archival footage, new filmed content, narrative texts and sound. The film explores the intertwined legacies of colonialism, the transatlantic slave trade and the climate crisis. It connects Barbadian poet Kamau Brathwaite's research on tidalectics – the notion of developing an oceanic worldview – and Christina Sharpe's concept of 'the wake', which illustrates how Black lives are bound up with and animated by the afterlives of slavery. *between a whisper and a cry* presents water as an archive of memory and trauma, and maps the entangled histories of empire and environmental catastrophe across bodies and borders, urging viewers to consider how these forces continue to shape our relationship to space, place and our own bodies.

HELEN CAMMOCK

***The Lay Shaft Drive is Down*, 2023**
2K video: 12′ 46
July–September 2024

The Lay Shaft Drive is Down reinterprets the artist's spoken word and sung performance that was commissioned by The Line in 2023 and staged at the House Mill during the *Tributaries* exhibition. The film considers the mills in relation to industry, waterways and hardship: the tie to the colonial relationships that bind both people and production through contentious, often violent, yet sometimes radical histories.

MADGE GILL

***Untitled*, c. 1930–54**
Original work: Ink and watercolour on postcard,
13.5 × 8.7 cm
Reproduction: Vinyl, 280 × 173 cm
June 2021–ongoing

This watercolour and ink drawing, originally a postcard, is installed at the back of the Miller's House and highlights Gill's interest in experimenting with colour and texture. It features a mysterious young woman, a recurring figure in Gill's work, though she never gave any indication of who the woman might be. Across the water, surrounded by the reflections of the windows, her expression creates space for quiet contemplation.

THOMAS J PRICE

***Network*, 2013**
Bronze
274.3 × 100 x 92 cm
May 2015–November 2019

Thomas J Price's practice engages with themes of representation and perception, playing with material, scale and detail in order to challenge viewers' expectations. All of Price's works share a fascination with people, body language, and expression, as well as an exploration of classic modes of Western art and his own Jamaican heritage. *Network* shows a young, casually dressed man looking at his mobile phone, a common sight in this digital age, yet in bronze at nine feet tall, he invites us to question who we choose to represent in public statuary.

Reaching Out, 2020
Bronze
290 x 90 x 86 cm
May 2020–June 2022

Reaching Out was installed during the pandemic at the same site as *Network*, shortly after its departure, presenting a conversation between the two works. *Reaching Out* depicts a young woman wearing everyday clothes, holding a mobile phone in her hands. She is a fictional character created from various references to serve as a psychological portrait. The work continues the artist's theme of balancing experiences of isolation and connectedness, while acknowledging the different ways in which technology mediates our lives.

PHAIDON

RON HASELDEN

Diver, 2012
Co-curated with Artwise
Mixed media
26.5 x 6 x 3 m
November 2022–ongoing

Diver is a light installation that depicts a figure diving into water and making a splash. The work uses an animation effect created by lighting each stage of movement in sequence. As part of the 2012 Cultural Olympiad, it was designed by Ron Haselden in collaboration with 600 London primary school children during a series of animation workshops focusing on sports and wellbeing. *Diver* is installed within walking distance of the London Aquatics Centre, and its launch on The Line marked the tenth anniversary of the London 2012 Olympic and Paralympic Games.

Three Mills Wall · River Weir

SOMANG LEE

***The Living Line*, 2022**
Reproductions from watercolour drawings
120gsm outdoor blueback paper
2.14 x 146 m
July 2022–September 2024

The Living Line visualised plants, birds and insects that can be found along the route of The Line, such as the common poppy, grey heron and the Jersey tiger moth. Lee's practice is informed by a love of nature and outdoor adventures. The installation provided intricate illustrations as well as information about local wildlife. During the development of the commission, Lee led workshops at Pudding Mill Allotments with students from Carpenters School. The drawings they created featured in The Botanical Gallery at the centre of the installation. By encouraging people to spend more time in nature, the installation sought to inspire people to engage with their local environment to motivate them to protect it for the future.

Kingfisher
Electric blue and orange birds that hunt along rivers and streams. Can be seen perched over the water hunting for fish.
When to see?
Year-round

MADGE GILL

Untitled, c. 1930–54
Original works: Ink on postcard, 13.5 x 8.7 cm (x10)
Reproductions: Dibond, 118.9 x 74.5 cm (x10)
June 2021–ongoing

The hardships Madge Gill endured in her life saw her turn to spiritualism and making, both providing relief from her mental turmoil. She was known to create over a hundred postcards in a single evening. Gill explained that this flurry of seemingly unending drawing activity was encouraged by a spirit guide she came to embody called Myrninerest. These ten black ink drawings, originally postcards, are installed in a Network Rail underpass at the southern entrance to Queen Elizabeth Olympic Park. The series features the repetitive patterns of flowers, swirling shapes, architectural forms and chequerboards that characterise her work.

ual:
BBC
Sadler's Wells

RASHEED ARAEEN

Discosailing: A Ballet on Water
Co-curated with Arup Phase 2
27 July 2024

Discosailing was first conceived in 1970 as both a work of art and a water sport. Araeen describes it as 'a system of sailing, or floating on water … performed individually or collectively involving many performers. [*Discosailing*] may appear as a sport but its underlying conception is the idea of a floating sculpture or sculptures. It can also be perceived as a form of live performance.' On 27 July 2024, to coincide with the first day of the Paris 2024 Olympics, community groups and members of the public participated in six thirty-minute performances that questioned the boundary that separates art from other activities of everyday life. Visitors to the Park encountered this meditative exploration of movement, with nine floating forms engaging with the natural forces of wind and water.

ANISH KAPOOR

***ArcelorMittal Orbit*, 2012**
Steel
Height 115 m
May 2012–ongoing

Commissioned by the Greater London Authority for the London 2012 Olympic and Paralympic Games

ArcelorMittal Orbit is the UK's tallest sculpture at 115 metres. Rising above Queen Elizabeth Olympic Park, the work is characterised by its looping, latticed and continually coiling structure that invites the viewer to move around and inside it. Made of painted red steel, the material nods to the industrial heritage of the area, while its form references the Tower of Babel. Kapoor has said, 'I wanted the sensation of instability, something that was continually in movement. Traditionally a tower is pyramidal in structure, but we have done quite the opposite, we have a flowing, coiling form that changes as you walk around it.'

CARSTEN HÖLLER

The Slide, 2016
Steel
Length 178 m
June 2016–ongoing

Commissioned by London Legacy Development Corporation

At 178 metres long, Carsten Höller's sleek, steel slide is the world's tallest and longest tunnel slide. Travelling at speeds of up to 24 kilometres per hour, visitors wind their way through Anish Kapoor's *ArcelorMittal Orbit*. Through the slide's transparent top sections, they can catch glimpses of Queen Elizabeth Olympic Park and London's skyline before being plunged into darkness. Höller, inspired by childhood memories and his fascination with slides, aims to inject fun and excitement into daily life. He notes, 'It's virtually impossible to go down a slide without smiling.'

MAHTAB HUSSAIN

***Please Take a Seat*, 2025**
102 × 187 × 90 cm
April 2025–ongoing

Please Take a Seat – a contemporary reinterpretation of a Victorian park bench – is an exploration of representation, identity and place. Developed by Mahtab Hussain in collaboration with The Line's Youth Collective, the engraved prompt 'Hello, let's make a portrait together' invites visitors to sit, reflect and use the bench as a prop to create their own portrait. This interaction will form a growing, collaborative portrait of East London, created by residents and visitors to Queen Elizabeth Olympic Park, that returns the bench to its historic role in activating civic space. The bench features selected motifs from the artist and the Youth Collective's research into the local area, including the Bow Bells, a grey heron and a microphone to represent Newham's association with grime music. Digitally scanned portraits of Youth Collective members are cast on the back panel of the bench.

ual:
V&A

Sadler's Wells

SPECIAL PROJECTS

The Line has been invited to commission projects at a number of locations adjacent to its main route. Working at London City Island and London City Airport presented a unique opportunity for The Line to engage with the public realm in different contexts, bringing them to life through colour and movement.

Detail: Anne Hardy, *Destination London*, 2021

PAUL HUXLEY & HOLLY ROWAN HESSON

Conversation in Colour
arebyte, London City Island
Curated by Royal Society of Sculptors
October 2018

Conversation in Colour was an exhibition that brought together Huxley's characteristic geometric abstraction and vivid use of colour with Hesson's sculptural interventions. For this site-specific show, Huxley created two new canvases that were juxtaposed with Hesson's installations, which used Perspex, projectors and overlapping coloured filter strips to create striking compositions. While the artists work in different media, they both use planes of colour to create visual riddles, and visitors were invited to take part in the dialogue inspired by the artists' work.

ANNE HARDY

Destination London, 2021
London City Airport
Vinyl
Four sections, full length: 3 x 39 m
August 2021–December 2023

Destination London was a series of large 2D installations located on four walls in the arrivals corridor at London City Airport. Originally developed as photograms and subsequently printed onto vinyl, the installation aimed to communicate a vivid sense of the layered histories of London, expressed through the diverse botanical life found around the airport, with samples collected by the artist herself. Through the series of imagined and atmospheric landscapes, visitors encountered the rich flora of the local area. When travelling, humans have always brought plants, seeds and roots with them, and the diversity of plant life reflected in this commission referenced these historical journeys.

RANA BEGUM

***No. 1104 Catching Colour*, 2022**
London City Island
Powder-coated mesh, steel and rope
26 x 36 x 6 m
April 2022–March 2024

Suspended above Botanic Square, Rana Begum's site-specific installation, *No. 1104 Catching Colour*, comprised clouds of brightly coloured mesh forms, creating a dynamic interplay of colour, light and shadow. The artist said, 'For me, it's about opening up people's eyes to the possibilities of their surroundings … [to] heighten their senses.'

To celebrate the launch of the work, The Line initiated a collaboration between Begum and English National Ballet, whose building is adjacent to the installation site. Building on the artist's long-standing collaboration with Roksanda Ilinčić, the dancers wore clothing by ROKSANDA. Choreographed by Stina Quagebeur, two dancers engaged in a dynamic exchange under Begum's installation, with music composed by award-winning composer Jeremy Birchall (see images overleaf). In parallel, two local secondary schools worked with English National Ballet and the South Asian dance company Akademi to develop a performance that fused Kathak, ballet and contemporary dance.

HERCULES

A SHORT HISTORY OF THE LINE'S ROUTE

GREENWICH PENINSULA

Greenwich Peninsula is on a prominent bend on the southern bank of the River Thames, opposite the Isle of Dogs, and marks the southernmost point of The Line's route.

The marshland here was drained and reclaimed in the sixteenth century by Dutch engineers who used it for pasture, and it remained an agricultural area, dotted with farmland plots and tidal marshes, for over two centuries.

Due to its position at the gateway to the city, Bugsby's Marsh (as it was known) gained notoriety in the seventeenth century for a gruesome spectacle. The bodies of pirates were transported here from Execution Dock in Wapping and were left to rot in cages that lined the river. 'Thames Tassels', as the gibbets were known, were a deterrent to any piracy-minded sailors and smugglers living and working along this stretch of river, and to any visitor arriving in London by sea.

The East Greenwich Gas Works dominated the peninsula in the nineteenth century. Constructed in 1880 by the South Metropolitan Gas Company, the gasworks grew to cover 150 acres and over a mile of river frontage. Gas production ceased in 1976 following the discovery of North Sea gas, and the enormous gasometer, affectionately nicknamed 'Jumbo' (which featured in Blur's 'Parklife' music video) was dismantled in 2020. Remnants of the coal jetty live on as part of North Greenwich Pier, with one section (or four columns) used as the base of Antony Gormley's *Quantum Cloud*.

Today the peninsula features one of the UK's most recognisable landmarks, The O2 (formerly the Millennium Dome). Designed by the Richard Rogers Partnership (now RSHP) under the direction of Mike Davies, the dome's design represents the measurements of time and speaks to its location on the Greenwich Meridian; its 365-metre diameter reflects the days of the year and its iconic yellow support towers reference twelve hours, twelve months, and the twelve zodiac constellations.

Before industrialisation, the wetlands here would have been teeming with wildlife. In recent years, river terraces and reed beds have been created along the banks of the Thames with the aim of emulating these habitats, which are now home to a large number of birds, including bittern. Two species of seal call the tidal Thames home – harbour and grey seals – with a combined population of around 3,500. They have been spotted at low tide on the sandbanks at Greenwich Peninsula (see page 66), and in Bow Creek as far north as Three Mills. Short-snouted seahorses have also been found living in the Thames, particularly in the area between Greenwich and the South Bank, and the river is home to an estimated 125 different species of fish.

VISIBLE FROM GREENWICH PENINSULA

Across the river, in the shadow of Canary Wharf, stands West India Docks. Built to handle goods like sugar, rum, coffee and timber from Caribbean slave plantations, West India Docks opened in 1802 and served as a crucial point in the British Empire's vast trade network for 180 years. Scottish merchant and slave trader Robert Milligan, who profited from trafficking enslaved Africans, was largely responsible for their construction. On 9 June 2020, his statue was removed from outside Museum of London Docklands, coinciding with the announcement of Mayor of London Sadiq Khan's Commission for Diversity in the Public Realm. This was established to review and assess public tributes, including statues and other landmarks, following the Black Lives Matter protests, and the subsequent toppling of the statue of slave trader Edward Colston.

With the advent of the shipping container, shipping operations moved downriver to Tilbury, and West India Docks closed in 1980. This was a time of social unrest and protests due to the major job losses across whole communities, the impact of which is still felt today. Shortly after the docks closed, their regeneration began, leading to today's financial district.

To the east of Canary Wharf is Trinity Buoy Wharf (see page 73), which is home to a vibrant creative community, event venues, and the original Container City. Nestled among them – adjacent to the mouth of the River Lea (Bow Creek) – is London's only surviving lighthouse, which was built in 1864. The Experimental Lighthouse, as it is known, was never used to aid navigation on the Thames but to experiment and develop lighting equipment for the Trinity House network of lighthouses, lightships and buoys, as well as to train lighthouse personnel.

The celebrated scientist Michael Faraday worked as scientific advisor to Trinity House from 1836 to 1865 and conducted many optical experiments there. Today, Trinity Buoy Wharf is home to the Faraday Effect, one of London's smallest museums, an immersive 'recreation' of Faraday's workshop. The lighthouse is home to Jem Finer's *Longplayer*, a thousand-year-long musical composition that began playing at midnight on 31 December 1999. It features the sound of singing bowls – an ancient type of standing bell still used in Buddhist and meditation practices

View of Greenwich Peninsula and The O2 with Antony Gormley's *Quantum Cloud* visible on the left and Richard Wilson's *A Slice of Reality* visible on the right (top), and Lascars Ave detail of Mahtab Hussain's *Please Take a Seat*

– and was originally produced as an Artangel commission. It is intended to play without repetition until the last moment of 2999, at which point it will complete its cycle and begin again.

ROYAL DOCKS
Royal Docks is an area in the London Borough of Newham, named after a collection of three docks: Royal Victoria Dock (opened in 1855), Royal Albert Dock (opened in 1880) and King George V Dock (opened in 1921). In their heyday, the three docks collectively formed the largest enclosed docks in the world. Hundreds of thousands of cargo ships unloaded grain, tobacco, silk, tea, fruits and vegetables here, much of it arriving from British colonies.

Newham has a rich history shaped by different groups of people arriving to work here, particularly since the nineteenth century. It's one of the most diverse boroughs in the UK and over 200 languages and dialects are spoken here today.

Lascars Avenue commemorates the history of sailors, particularly those from the Indian subcontinent, who served on European ships. Lascars were employed using Asiatic agreements which defined the conditions of their employment. They were paid a fraction of the wages of their European counterparts, which meant their employment increased profits and contributed towards the prosperity of the British Empire. By 1914, lascars made up 17.5 per cent of the total number of mariners on British registered ships. At times, whole crews consisted of lascars. They faced significant discrimination and were cruelly treated. Lascars Avenue serves as a reminder of the history of these sailors and their contributions to British shipping and the cultural diversity of the area. Lascars Avenue is immortalised on Mahtab Hussain's bench, *Please Take a Seat* (see opposite page).

Over 25,000 bombs were dropped on London's docklands during World War II as the warehouses, railways, and factories were critical to Britain's war effort. They recovered after the war but suffered a steady decline from the 1960s onwards following the introduction of containerisation. The last commercial ships left these docks in 1981, which had a devastating impact on employment – and the community – locally. Their regeneration began shortly after and London City Airport opened in 1987, University of East London (Docklands Campus) in 1999, the Excel exhibition centre in 2000, and London Cable Car in 2012.

In 2022, the Mayor of London and the London Assembly officially moved into the new City Hall in the Royal Docks and the Elizabeth line opened, providing rapid access from across London. The Mayor's move is part of a wider investment programme intending to act as a catalyst for the further regeneration of the docks. The building was originally designed by WilkinsonEyre as a global sustainability showcase. When it opened in 2012, 'The Crystal' (as it was then known) was the world's first building to achieve the highest possible ratings of BREEAM and LEED sustainable construction standards, embodying innovative approaches to minimising energy, carbon and water consumption.

City Hall is located on Kamal Chunchie Way, which is named after the Sri Lankan-born Methodist minister Kamal Athon Chunchie, who founded the Coloured Men's Institute in the Royal Docks in 1926. Chunchie established the institute for sailors, dock workers, and local residents in response to the racism that Black and Asian communities suffered in Canning Town. Through the institute, he fought for the rights of minorities in the UK, and the new name of the road (previously Siemens Brothers Way) was chosen by the public in 2021.

Although much of the original dock infrastructure has been redeveloped, the skyline is still defined by two architectural icons of post-industrial Britain: the Tate & Lyle factory and Millennium Mills. There are also fourteen iconic Stothert & Pitt cranes located in pairs along the north and south docksides. The westernmost pair on the south side are the earliest, possibly from the 1920s, and the rest date from 1962.

STAR LANE – CODY DOCK
Cody Dock is situated on the River Lea, near Star Lane station, approximately halfway between Queen Elizabeth Olympic Park and Greenwich Peninsula.

Originally built in 1871, Cody Dock was constructed by the Imperial Chemical Company to serve as a coal unloading dock for the nearby Bromley-by-Bow Gasworks, and to distribute the factory's many byproducts, such as soap and the pigment Prussian Blue. The Gaslight and Coke Company later purchased the dock, and it was last used by British Gas before falling into a state of disrepair in the 1960s.

Cody Dock was partially filled in and for three decades was used as a dumping ground for hundreds of cubic metres of fly-tipped waste, leaving it blocked off and preventing access to the eastern side of the River Lea.

One (unsubstantiated) line of thought is that Cody Dock gained its name from the camp that William Frederick Cody, better known as Buffalo Bill, set up while touring. Ahead of his Wild West Show at Earl's Court, which formed part of the celebrations for Queen Victoria's Golden Jubilee year, he docked at Gravesend in Kent on 14 April 1887. Colonel Cody proceeded directly to London and the rest of the company sailed up the Thames, disembarking at Royal Albert Dock the following morning, about three miles east of here.

Led by Simon Myers, Gasworks Dock Partnership, a charity dedicated to the community-led restoration of Cody Dock, was formed in 2009. With funding from trusts and foundations, support from Thames Water and a team of over 3,500 devoted volunteers, thousands of tonnes of waste were cleared from the site and Cody Dock opened to the public with regular hours in 2015, coinciding with the opening of The Line. Their ten-year masterplan launched in 2018 and includes the creation of artist studios, a visitor centre, moorings, a heritage pavilion and therapeutic gardens.

In 2022, Cody Dock launched its award-winning Rolling Bridge, designed by Thomas Randall-Page. Ordinarily, the bridge serves as a crossing for pedestrians and cyclists, but it can rotate 180 degrees to allow boats to pass beneath, supporting the wider ambition to reopen the dock as a site for boat restoration.

Cody Dock has championed access to the River Lea and facilitated an awareness and understanding of the biodiversity and rich industrial heritage of the area. It offers an unexpected oasis after the journey through the industrial estates between Star Lane station and the river. Its citizen scientist programme of birdwatching has recorded ninety-seven species of birds along the river, including redstarts and green woodpeckers. Kingfishers are a regular sight at Cody Dock, too.

The local area will see significant change over the coming decades as part of Newham's regeneration plans. At the time of writing, Cody Dock is the southernmost accessible part of the River Lea's path, but plans are underway to open it up further south; in due course, there will be a continuous river path to the Thames.

RIVER LEA

The River Lea, London's second largest river, originates in the Chiltern Hills in Bedfordshire and flows south east for some forty-two miles before meeting the River Thames. In the Roman period, the river was recorded as being a wide, fast-flowing watercourse surrounded by marshland. During the Middle Ages, millers made use of the river's power, establishing water mills to produce flour for city bakers.

The first act for improving a river was granted by parliament in 1424, when the River Lee Commissioners were charged with improving navigation through the watercourse. Over the next few centuries, works were regularly carried out to speed up transport, including creating towpaths, making new cuts, dredging the river and constructing locks.

The oldest brick building in London is believed to be Bromley Hall, which is visible from the edge of the river by Abigail Fallis's *DNA DL90* (see opposite page). Built in 1485, it was a rural retreat for John Blount, courtier to Henry VIII, whose daughter, Elizabeth – a lady-in-waiting to Catherine of Aragon – became the King's mistress and mother to his only recognised illegitimate son. The hall has changed hands many times over the centuries, but from the 1680s to the 1820s it was owned by various members of a distinguished Quaker family, who developed it into one of the largest calico printing factories on the River Lea. The origins of the East End textile industry can be traced to the fourteenth century when Flemish artisans set up dye works on the River Lea. From the 1600s, the river supported textile-related industries, including dyeing and silk weaving, and in the late 1600s, the silk industry was replaced by calico printing, with suggestions that the first calico printer in England was William Sherwin of West Ham.

The area maintained its largely rural character until the nineteenth century, when the Lower Lea Valley became a hub for the chemical, ink and confectionery industries, among others. The river's proximity to London and easy navigation made it an important transport route for all manner of goods, including flour, textiles and, later, machinery.

Seven giant gas holders – located on the eastern bank of the River Lea by Twelvetrees Crescent – are a prominent feature in the landscape of this section of The Line's route. They were originally part of the Bromley-by-Bow Gasworks and built by the Imperial Gas Light and Coke Company in the 1870s. The gas holders' surrounds are cast iron and the central drums are steel. They are intricately decorated, with a different repeating pattern on each storey. There were originally nine gas holders, but several were damaged when the site was bombed in 1940. The surviving seven are

View of Bromley Hall (the red brick building to the right) and Canary Wharf

Grade II listed (individually and collectively) and represent the largest group of Victorian gas holders in the UK (two are visible on page 154).

Once considered one of the UK's most polluted rivers, the Lower Lea was shut off to the public for decades. In spite of its long association with industry and for conveying domestic and industrial effluence into the Thames, and the ongoing challenges posed by sewage outflows, concerted efforts to clean up and restore wildlife to London's second river are well underway. A partnership between Thames 21, Cody Dock and the Environment Agency led to riparian habitat works and the installation of new reed beds, which improve water quality, support wildlife and restore the river's ecological health. Dragonflies, damselflies, carp, grey herons, little egrets, kingfishers, swans, coots and moorhens all make a home in this industrial landscape.

THREE MILLS ISLAND

Three Mills Island is a teardrop-shaped pocket of land surrounded by the Channelsea River, Three Mills Wall River, and the Prescott Channel.

The Domesday Survey of 1086 recorded at least eight tidal mills here, making the River Lea's mills among the earliest tidal mills recorded in England. Powered by holding back the high tide within a fifty-seven-acre mill pond (which stretched across the site of the current Queen Elizabeth Olympic Park, as far back as Lea Bridge Road), the mills could work up to eight hours in each of the two daily tides, making them some of London's biggest producers of milled grain. Three Mills takes its name from the world's largest surviving tidal mill, the Grade I listed House Mill, and the Clock Mill next door, notable for its clock tower and distinctive conical roofs. The third mill, a windmill, was destroyed in 1840. Transformed in the eighteenth century into a large gin distillery complex in (what is now) 3 Mills Studios, the mills went from producing flour to milling grain for gin production, fuelling the gin palaces of London's 'gin craze', and even supplying the Royal Navy. Mash from the gin was used to feed large farms of pigs whose bones supplied the china factories at Bow, while their fat was used by local soap makers.

The historic architecture and cobbled paths that surround the buildings are in stark contrast to the six lanes of traffic that constitute the A12, which runs 200 metres to the west of this enchanting enclave.

On the eastern edge of Three Mills Green, across the Prescott Channel, the grand cupola of Abbey Mills Pumping Station pokes out of the trees (see opposite page). Dubbed the 'Cathedral of Sewage' for its ornate Victorian design, the pumping station was a key component of Joseph Bazalgette's sewage system. Still in use today, it is part of The Thames Tideway Tunnel, a deep-level 'super sewer' that transports waste all the way from Acton in West London through Abbey Mills here in the east, and finally to Beckton Sewage Treatment Works.

Just north of Three Mills Island is the Greenway, which stands over a giant sewer. Built between 1860 and 1865, the Northern Outfall Sewer was part of Joseph Bazalgette's network of over 1,300 miles [2,090 kilometres] of brick sewers, designed as a solution for London's chronic drainage and sewerage problems. The embankment over the Northern Outfall Sewer is 4.5 miles [7.2 kilometres] long and has long been used as a footpath. It was formerly known as 'Sewerbank' and in 1931 it became the temporary haunt of Mahatma Gandhi, who spent three months at Kingsley Hall, less than half a mile west of Three Mills Island, for discussions on the future of colonial India. He liked to take early-morning walks along Sewerbank as it offered elevated views and a chance to meet local well-wishers.

Like much of East London, Three Mills Island sustained serious bomb damage during World War II, including the Miller's House, and by the 1950s the mills had ceased operations. In the 1970s, the House Mill was slated for demolition and the House Mill Trust was formed to save and restore the buildings. In recent years, the Miller's House has been rebuilt and the fabric of the House Mill has been restored, allowing it to function as an important heritage centre that also hosts a café, events and The Line's film exhibitions.

Adjacent to the House Mill, the Clock Mill is the current (temporary) home of the Harris Science Academy East London. The former gin distillery, 3 Mills Studio, is an iconic centre for film and television production that has been used by filmmakers including Wes Anderson and Tim Burton, as well as a rehearsal space by English National Opera, among others. Collectively, they are a thriving hub of heritage, education and creativity at Three Mills Island.

View of Abbey Mills Pumping Station across Three Mills Green

QUEEN ELIZABETH OLYMPIC PARK

Queen Elizabeth Olympic Park is at the intersection of the London boroughs of Tower Hamlets, Newham, Hackney and Waltham Forest and marks the top of The Line's route.

Once a sparsely populated landscape of marshes, wild vegetation, canals, locks, bridges, towpaths and pylons, the waterways surrounding and flowing through what is now Queen Elizabeth Olympic Park were used to transport flour, timber and various industrial goods to and from factories and distilleries in Hackney Wick and Old Ford.

Stratford was once home to Stratford Works, a major locomotive building works depot. In 1891, the site made headlines by building a freight engine in just nine-and-a-half hours, setting a world record, and drawing crowds and newspaper coverage. During World War II, Stratford Works played a crucial role in building aircraft components and artillery parts, even in the face of bombing raids. The final part of the works closed in 1991 and the site is now home to Westfield shopping centre.

Tens of thousands of construction workers cleared 560 acres of land in preparation for the London 2012 Olympic and Paralympic Games; derelict factories, industrial estates and homes were demolished, pylons were removed, overhead electricity cables were buried beneath the ground, and contaminated soil and waterways were painstakingly cleaned up.

Workers taking soil samples uncovered remnants of the site's industrial heritage: bottles, clay pipes and shrapnel. Where the London Aquatics Centre now stands, archaeologists uncovered an Iron Age settlement and an ancient burial ground containing four skeletons, the remains of which are thought to be over 3,000 years old.

Today, the London Stadium, London Aquatics Centre and other venues across the site host major sporting events and concerts, while the Park itself features thousands of trees, wetland and perennial plants, and vast expanses of meadow. The 2012 Olympic Gardens feature 70,000 plants from 250 different species and are divided into climatic zones – Europe, North America, the Southern Hemisphere and Asia – each drawing upon the plant communities and ecological character of habitats found in the wild.

East Bank is located at the northernmost part of The Line's route; a new cultural quarter for innovation, creativity and learning that began opening in autumn 2023. It brings together BBC Music Studios; London College of Fashion, UAL; Sadler's Wells East; UCL (University College London) and V&A East to create a world-class cultural destination that is a powerful legacy of the London 2012 Olympic and Paralympic Games.

ARTIST BIOGRAPHIES

LARRY ACHIAMPONG (b. 1984, London, UK)
Larry Achiampong's solo and collaborative projects explore class, cross-cultural identity and the post-digital era through imagery, live performance, and aural and visual archives. His work examines personal and communal heritage and the intersection of pop culture and the post-colonial experience. He has exhibited at Tate Britain (2021), Somerset House (2019), and the Venice and Singapore Biennales (2017 and 2019 respectively). He received the Paul Hamlyn Award for Artists (2019), the Stanley Picker Fellowship (2020), and in 2022, Turner Contemporary presented his first major solo exhibition. In 2025, Tate published his monograph, *If It Don't Exist, Build It*.

RASHEED ARAEEN (b. 1935, Karachi, Pakistan)
Born and educated in Karachi, Rasheed Araeen trained as an engineer before moving to Europe in the 1960s to become one of the pioneers of Minimalist sculpture in Britain. He founded the groundbreaking journal *Third Text* and, in 1989, curated the first major retrospective of work by Asian and African artists in Britain, *The Other Story: Afro-Asian Artists in Post-War Britain* at the Hayward Gallery. His work is included in public and private collections, and a recent retrospective of his work toured from Van Abbemuseum, Netherlands (2017–18) to MAMCO, Switzerland (2018); Baltic, UK (2018–19); and the Garage Museum of Contemporary Art, Russia (2019). His installation *Zero to Infinity* was the Uniqlo Tate Play commission in the Turbine Hall in 2023.

MARTHA ATIENZA (b. 1981, Manila, Philippines)
Martha Atienza lives and works in Bantayan Island in the Philippines. Her practice is rooted in her ecological and cultural concerns, as she studies the intricate interplay between local traditions, human subjectivity, society and the environment. Atienza's work has gained international recognition with her piece *Our Islands* earning her the Baloise Art Prize at Art Basel in 2017. She has also been awarded the Ateneo Art Awards in Manila in 2012 and 2016, as well as the Cultural Center of the Philippines Thirteen Artist Award in 2015. Her work has been exhibited internationally, including at the Istanbul Biennial (2022), Bangkok Art Biennale (2020), Honolulu Biennial (2019), and Asia Pacific Triennial of Contemporary Art (2018–19). In 2022, her solo exhibition *The Protectors* inaugurated Silverlens in New York.

JAMES BALMFORTH (b. 1980, Plymouth, UK)
James Balmforth is a London-based artist whose sculptural works explore material transformation and balance. He studied at Chelsea College of Art & Design, graduating in 2003. His work has been exhibited at the Venice Biennale, Royal Academy of Arts, Cass Sculpture Foundation and Bold Tendencies. Solo exhibitions include Celine, New York (2019), Robilant+Voena, Milan (2016), and Hannah Barry Gallery, London (2016, 2011 and 2009).

RANA BEGUM (b. 1977, Sylhet, Bangladesh)
Rana Begum's work focuses on the interplay between light and colour and blurs the boundaries between sculpture, painting and architecture. Her drawings, paintings, wall-based sculptures and large-scale public art projects are influenced by the geometric abstraction of Minimalism and Constructivism. She has exhibited widely in the UK and abroad, including at Pitzhanger Gallery and Manor, London (2022); Wanas Konst, Sweden (2021); Kettle's Yard, Cambridge (2018); and Tate St Ives (2018). Begum was elected as a Royal Academician in 2020. She lives and works in London.

URSULA BIEMANN (b. 1955, Zurich, Switzerland)
Ursula Biemann is an artist, author and video essayist. Her practice is research oriented and involves fieldwork in diverse locales from Greenland to Amazonia, where she investigates climate change and the ecologies of oil, ice, forests and water. She published *Forest Mind* with Spector Books (2022), and an audio-visual online monograph about her ecological video works from 2011–21, titled *Becoming Earth*. Biemann has had recent solo exhibitions at MUAC, Mexico City (2024) and MQ Freiraum, Vienna (2024). Her work has also featured in international art biennials and major museum exhibitions worldwide. She received the 2009 Prix Meret Oppenheim.

HELEN CAMMOCK (b. 1970, Staffordshire, UK)
Helen Cammock is a London- and Wales-based artist whose multi-disciplinary practice spans film, photography, print, text and performance. Central to her practice is the voice: the uncovering of marginalised voices within history, the question of who speaks on behalf of whom and on what terms, and how her own voice reflects in different ways on the stories explored in her work. Recent solo shows include *Helen Cammock: I Will Keep My Soul at Art + Practice*, Los Angeles, and Rivers Institute for Contemporary Art & Thought, New Orleans (2023), and *Bass Notes and SiteLines* at Amant, Brooklyn (2023). Cammock was a joint winner of the Turner Prize in 2019 and winner of the 7th edition of the Max Mara Art Prize for Women in 2017.

ALEX CHINNECK (b. 1984, Bedford, UK)
Alex Chinneck works across the fields of art, architecture

and theatre. Known for unzipping the facades of buildings, tying knots in pillars and postboxes, and gravity-defying installations, his public artworks and sculptures playfully disrupt the world around us. Chinneck's installations have been featured across the UK and internationally, including *A Week at the Knees* (Clerkenwell Design Week, 2025), *Rock and Roll* (Milan Design Week, 2019) and *Pick Yourself Up and Pull Yourself Together* (Southbank Centre, 2015). He is a member of the Royal Society of Sculptors and lives and works in Kent.

SERGE ATTUKWEI CLOTTEY (b. 1984, Accra, Ghana)
Serge Attukwei Clottey works with found materials from his hometown in Accra, Ghana, in order to create a dialogue with the city's cultural history and identity. He uses everyday objects like discarded Kufuor gallons, car tyres and boat wood, uplifting these materials into symbols of Ghana's vernacular economic system of trade and reuse. Recent projects have included his large-scale 'Afrogallonism' installations, including *The Golden Falls* for Desert X 2022 in AlUla, Saudi Arabia, and *Shooting For Hunger*, an installation for the *Food Forever* programme at Kew Gardens (2022).

MARTIN CREED (b. 1968, Wakefield, UK)
Martin Creed is an artist, composer and performer. His artworks, objects, statements, suggestions and performances are minimal and are identified only by numbers. He uses commonplace materials – like tape, balloons and Blu-Tac – and minimal intervention to draw our attention to things that we might otherwise overlook. In 2001, he won the Turner Prize for *Work No. 227: The lights going on and off*, a piece in which electric lights turn on and off, illuminating and darkening a room. His work is included in numerous public collections, and he has exhibited extensively worldwide, including solo exhibitions at the Orange County Museum of Art (2024), Museum für Konkrete Kunst (2023), Tate Modern (2018) and Hayward Gallery (2014).

TRACEY EMIN (b. 1963, London, UK)
Tracey Emin uses personal experience, memories and emotions to create frank and poetic, intimate and universal works of art. Her work has been exhibited in solo and group exhibitions around the world, including *Tracey Emin / Edvard Munch: The Loneliness of the Soul* at the Royal Academy, London (2021), *The Fear of Loving* at Musée d'Orsay, Paris (2019), and *Sex and Solitude* at Fondazione Palazzo Strozzi, Florence (2025). In 1999, she was nominated for the Turner Prize and famously exhibited *My Bed* (1998). In 2007, Emin represented Great Britain at the Venice Biennale, and she was elected a Royal Academician in the same year. In 2023, she opened TKE (Tracey Karima Emin) Studios in Margate and in 2024 was honoured with a Damehood for her services to art.

SIMON FAITHFULL (b. 1966, Ipsden, UK)
Simon Faithfull's work explores the planet as a sculptural object, testing its limits and reporting from its extremities through video, digital drawing, installation and writing. Notable projects include *Liverpool-to-Liverpool* (2010), a permanent public artwork at Lime Street Station that features 181 drawings made during a journey by container ship, train and bus from Liverpool (UK) to Liverpool (Nova Scotia). Faithfull's work is held in the collections of Centre Pompidou and the Arts Council. He lives and works in Berlin and is a professor at Slade School of Fine Art, London.

ABIGAIL FALLIS (b. 1968, London, UK)
Abigail Fallis experiments with diverse, often recycled, materials including papier mâché, everyday objects, fish skeletons, neon and bronze. She refers to her sculptures as 'thinking tools' and her work combines searching questions – about contemporary life, the environment and our consumerism – with her sense of humour. Fallis has exhibited widely throughout the UK and her work can be found in a number of public and private collections, including Damien Hirst's Murderme collection and the former Hix restaurants. In 2016, Fallis became a member of the Royal Society of Sculptors. She lives and works in Gloucestershire.

LAURA FORD (b. 1961, Cardiff, UK)
Laura Ford works with soft fabrics, materials, found objects, ceramics and bronze to create depictions of imagined or fantastical characters. Her sculptures are ostensibly sweet, though she overrides any notion of sentimentality by placing these anthropomorphic sculptures in situations that signal the unease and potential violence of socio-political power struggles. Ford has exhibited widely in the UK and internationally, including representing Wales at the Venice Biennale in 2005. Her work can be found in numerous public collections, including Tate and the Victoria & Albert Museum.

MADGE GILL (b. 1882, London, UK; d. 1961)
Madge Gill was a self-taught artist known for her ink drawings, textiles and embroideries. Born in Walthamstow, London, she had a turbulent childhood and was sent to Canada at the age of fourteen under the British Home

Children scheme. After returning to London, she married and had three sons, suffering several tragedies that affected her health. It was during this period that she began creating art, guided by a spirit she called Myrninerest. During her lifetime, she exhibited multiple times at the East End Academy at Whitechapel Gallery (1932–47) and The Wallace Collection (1942). More recently, her work has been exhibited at the Barbican (*Jean Dubuffet: Brutal Beauty*, 2021), Venice Biennale (2024), and The Wallace Collection (*Grayson Perry: Delusions of Grandeur*, 2025). In 2019, William Morris Gallery presented a solo exhibition of her work.

ANTONY GORMLEY (b. 1950, London, UK)
Antony Gormley is widely acclaimed for his sculptures, Installations and public artworks. His work investigates the relationship of the human body to space and asks fundamental questions about where human beings stand in relation to nature and the cosmos. Gormley's work has been exhibited at major venues, including the Musée Rodin, Paris (2023–24), the Uffizi Gallery, Florence (2019), and the Philadelphia Museum of Art (2019). His works *Angel of the North* and *Another Place* are on permanent display in Gateshead and Crosby, respectively. Gormley won the Turner Prize in 1994, was elected as a Royal Academician in 2003, and was awarded a Knighthood in 2014 for his services to the arts. He was made a Companion of Honour in 2025.

ANNE HARDY (b. 1970, St Albans, UK)
Anne Hardy is internationally recognised for her large-scale sculptural installations: immersive, sensual works that combine physical materials with lighting and surround sound. These works derive from places she calls 'pockets of wild space' – gaps in the urban space where materials, atmospheres and emotions gather. Hardy has exhibited at major institutions in the UK and Europe, including Fondazione Merz, Turin (2022); Museum Boijmans van Beuningen, Rotterdam (2018); Modern Art, Oxford (2015–16); and Secession, Vienna (2012). In 2019, she presented *The Depth of Darkness, the Return of the Light* for Tate Britain's Winter Commission.

RON HASELDEN (b. 1944, Gravesend, UK)
Ron Haselden works with light, sound, film and video, often as part of architectural projects. His three-dimensional works range from a minute scale to large performance productions involving up to 400 participants, which take place in major cities in Europe and elsewhere. Haselden has shown in many major international galleries and was awarded the Sargant Fellowship at the British School at Rome. He has received awards and grants from numerous funding bodies, and his work is represented in many private and public collections. He lives and works in London and in Plouër-sur-Rance, France.

HOLLY ROWAN HESSON (b. 1971, Berkshire, UK)
Holly Rowan Hesson is an artist and researcher working with installation, sculpture and photography. She creates altered visual and sensory works responding to the experience of physical space, architecture and the built environment. She has exhibited in solo and group shows across the UK. Solo exhibitions include *Echo*, commissioned by Warrington Contemporary Arts Festival, Pyramid Arts Centre (2017), *New Work* at &Model, Leeds, which followed a month-long residency (2016), and *Assembly*, Bankley Gallery, Manchester (2016), which was awarded after winning the Bankley Gallery Open.

DAMIEN HIRST (b. 1965, Bristol, UK)
Damien Hirst is an artist and art collector. He creates installations, sculptures, paintings and drawings that examine the complex relationships between art and beauty, religion and science, and life and death. His work is strongly identified with the YBAs who came to prominence in the early 1990s. From serialised paintings of multi-coloured spots to animal specimens preserved in tanks of formaldehyde, his work challenges contemporary belief systems, tracing the uncertainties that lie at the heart of human experience. Since 1987, his work has featured in more than eighty solo exhibitions and has been included in more than 260 group exhibitions that have taken place around the world.

CARSTEN HÖLLER (b. 1961, Brussels, Belgium)
Carsten Höller trained as a scientist before starting to make art in the late 1980s. He applies his training as a scientist to his work as an artist, concentrating on the nature of human relationships and the intersection of art, science and play. His works have included slides, carousels, animals, revolving doors and giant mushrooms, and frequently invite active participation. Major solo exhibitions include *Doubt*, Pirelli HangarBicocca, Milan (2016), *Decision*, Hayward Gallery, London (2015), *Experience*, New Museum, New York (2011), *Soma*, Hamburger Bahnhof, Berlin (2010) and *Test Site*, Tate Modern, London (2006).

GARY HUME (b. 1962, Pembury, UK)
Gary Hume is best known for his figurative and abstract paintings, which often feature striking colour combinations

made with premixed paints purchased from a hardware store. Hume's work is strongly identified with the YBAs who came to prominence in the early 1990s. He attended Goldsmiths College and went on to represent Britain at the São Paulo Biennial in 1996 – the same year he was nominated for the Turner Prize – and the Venice Biennale in 1999. Hume has exhibited widely, including solo shows at the Aspen Art Museum (2016), Tate Britain (2013), and Modern Art Oxford (2008). In 2001, he was elected a Royal Academician. Since 2017, he has exhibited new work in London, Belgium, New York, Berlin, Los Angeles, and Seoul.

MAHTAB HUSSAIN (b. 1981, Glasgow, UK)
Mahtab Hussain's work explores the important relationship between identity, heritage and displacement. His themes develop through long-term research articulating a visual language that challenges the prevailing concepts of multi-culturalism. Hussain has been the recipient of numerous awards and commissions and has published four artist books. His *You Get Me?* series was first presented at Autograph ABP, London in 2017, curated by Mark Sealy, and his critically acclaimed exhibition, *What Did You Want To See?*, opened at Ikon Gallery, Birmingham in 2025. He is currently working on an ongoing photo series, *Muslims in America*, which explores the diversity of American Muslim experience, connectedness and the power of community.

PAUL HUXLEY (b. 1938, London, UK)
Paul Huxley is a British painter known for his pioneering abstract works. His *Fluid* series influenced the genre of new abstract painting, while his *Key* series was crucial to the development of the divided canvases that have characterised his work ever since. Huxley's work has been exhibited worldwide, including solo shows at the Mark Rothko Centre, Latvia (2016), and the Azerbaijan Pavilion at the Venice Biennale (2015). A former professor of painting at the Royal College of Art, he has mentored many notable British artists and has been a Royal Academician since 1987. His monograph was published by Lund Humphries in 2024, which includes an extensive critical essay by Jeremy Lewison and chronology by Hester Westley.

YINKA ILORI MBE (b. 1987, London, UK)
Yinka Ilori MBE is a multi-disciplinary artist and designer whose bold visual language draws on his British-Nigerian heritage to convey new narratives through contemporary design. Drawing on Nigerian parables and verbal traditions, Ilori touches on themes that resonate with a global audience. He often uses the city as his canvas, reimagining spaces to encourage a sense of community and inviting audiences to engage and participate in his work and its surroundings. Major recent commissions include *Reflection in Numbers*, a striking pavilion in Berlin, Germany (2024), *Good Things Come to Those Who Wait*, a vibrant public art installation in Piccadilly Circus, London (2024), and *The Flamboyance of Flamingos*, a wildlife-inspired playground on the Becontree Estate, London (2022). Ilori's work has also been showcased globally, including Art Basel, Miami Beach (2024), Frieze Art Fair, Seoul (2023), and a solo exhibition at the Design Museum, London (2022–23). He was awarded an MBE in 2021 for his services to design.

ANISH KAPOOR (b. 1954, Mumbai, India)
Anish Kapoor works at vastly different scales and uses a diverse range of materials, from immense PVC skins, concave and convex mirrors, pigmented recesses carved in stone, and blood-red wax sculptures. He has exhibited extensively, and his work is included in museum collections around the world. He represented Britain at the 44th Venice Biennale in 1990 with *Void Field* (1989), for which he was awarded the Premio Duemila for Best Young Artist. He won the Turner Prize in 1991, was elected as a Royal Academician in 1999, and was awarded a Knighthood in 2013 for his services to visual arts.

SOMANG LEE (b. 1982, Stuttgart, Germany)
Somang Lee is an award-winning illustrator and projection artist based in London. Her creative practice is informed by her love of the natural world and outdoor adventures. Her aim is to create illustrations that are both beautiful and useful – making use of the wonder of nature to inspire others to get out there and be part of it. Previous projects include commissions for Towner Eastbourne (2021), Museum of London Archaeology (2020), Serpentine Galleries (2019), Shindagha Museum (2016), and Royal Botanical Gardens at Kew (2015).

HANNA LJUNGH (b. 1974, Washington DC, USA)
Hanna Ljungh works with film, photography, sculpture and installation. Ljungh devotes particular attention to the matter we call stone, soil, land, earth, and contemplates such notions as the Anthropocene, the distribution of resources, and what people are ultimately made of. Ljungh's work has been shown at Moderna Museet, Malmö (2019); Kunsthall Trondheim (2018); Studio Hippolyte and HIAP, Helsinki (2014); Kumho Museum of Art, Seoul (2014); and the Swedish Cultural Institute, Paris (2009). Her work is included in several private collections and can be found at Moderna Museet in Stockholm, the city in which she lives and works.

DANIELA MEDINA POCH (b. 1992, Bogotá, Colombia) & ELIZABETH GALLÓN DROSTE (b. 1991, Bogotá, Colombia)
Daniela Medina Poch is a researcher, artist and educator, currently part of the curatorial team at Gropius Bau. From an intersectional and plural perspective, her work explores unofficial histories, non-hegemonic forms of knowledge and systems of reciprocity to reimagine kinship, governance and communication across species. A Goldrausch fellow (2023) and nominee for the Rainer Wild Prize (2025), she has presented her work at institutions and events including MUDAM, Luxembourg (2025), The I and III Listening Biennial, Berlin (2021 and 2025), the XXII Cerveira Biennial, Portugal (2022), TBA21 Academy, Ocean Space Online (2022), and documenta fifteen, Kassel (2022). Her work is part of the permanent collections of MAMBO, Bogotá and the digital collection of the Museum of Historical Memory of Bogotá. She is the founder of the climate justice platform Embodied Climate Agency and co-founder of Babel Media Art.

Elizabeth Gallón Droste is a postdoctoral researcher at the Center for Spatial Cosmology, HafenCity University Hamburg. Her work bridges artistic research and anthropology through the arts of listening, with a focus on fluvial ecologies, socio-environmental conflicts and the re-mediations of extractive landscapes. She holds a PhD in Anthropology from Freie Universität Berlin (2024) with *Voicing Rivers Atrato*. Since 2022, she has been part of the artistic duo ~pes, attuning to subterranean and interstitial worlds through sonic evocations, and since 2025, she is a member of The Listening Academy. She has participated in RAW Material, Dakar (2024), *Meandering* at TBA21 Academy, Córdoba (2023), and documenta fifteen, Kassel (2022). Her publications include the book *Útica, Under the Murmuring Waters* (Oreri, 2024).

VIRGINIA OVERTON (b. 1971, Nashville, USA)
Virginia Overton is an American artist whose practice comprises installation, sculpture and photography. She often selects recycled objects that are found on site or things discovered in the environs of the exhibition space. Wood, metal, Plexiglas and fluorescent lighting – materials more commonly associated with architecture, construction work or farming – are cut, bent and hammered into works that evince the power and sensory quality of their own materials. Recent solo exhibitions include Kunst Museum Winterthur, Switzerland (2025); Landcraft Garden Foundation, New York (2023); Hypermaremma, Italy (2023); Frist Art Museum, Nashville (2022); and Goldsmiths CCA, London (2022). Overton lives and works in New York.

EDUARDO PAOLOZZI (b. 1924, Leith, UK; d. 2005)
Pop artist Eduardo Paolozzi was a sculptor and printmaker. He produced large-scale figurative sculptures, prints and collages made from magazines and other found objects. His large-scale public commissions transformed spaces including the British Library courtyard and London Underground's Tottenham Court Road station. His works are held in many public collections, including the National Galleries of Scotland, Edinburgh; the Museum of Modern Art, New York; and Tate, London.

THOMAS J PRICE (b. 1981, London, UK)
Thomas J Price works across disciplines including photography, performance and sculpture. He is known for his large-scale sculptures that depict everyday people. In 2020, Price was commissioned by Hackney Council to honour the Windrush Generation with a public sculpture that was unveiled in June 2022. He has exhibited widely in the UK and internationally, including solo shows at Museo Novecento, Florence (2025), the Power Plant, Toronto (2019), National Portrait Gallery, London (2016), and Yorkshire Sculpture Park (2014). His work is included in a number of public and private collections, including National Gallery of Victoria, Melbourne, Australia; Studio Museum in Harlem, New York; and the Rennie Collection in Canada.

JOANNA RAJKOWSKA (b. 1968, Bydgoszcz, Poland)
Joanna Rajkowska works with objects, film and photography. She is best known for her works in public space, which include performative and participatory projects and installations, often taking non-human animals and the natural world as their subject. Rajkowska has exhibited widely in the UK and internationally. Her public projects include commissions by the United Nations Environment Programme, Poland (2019) and the Berlin Biennale, Germany (2012). Rajkowska lives and works in Warsaw and London.

EVA ROTHSCHILD (b. 1971, Dublin, Republic of Ireland)
Eva Rothschild works with a wide range of materials including plaster, painted steel, leather, wood, tiles and paper. Her work has developed out of the legacy of the modernist sculptural tradition and a commitment to sculpture's capacity to create bodily encounters in space. She has exhibited worldwide, including at the Australian Centre for Contemporary Art, Melbourne (2018), Hepworth Wakefield (2011) and Tate Britain (2009). In 2014, Rothschild was elected as a Royal Academician, and in 2019 she represented Ireland at the 58th Venice Biennale. She lives and works in East London.

STERLING RUBY (b. 1972, Bitburg, Germany)
Sterling Ruby is an American/Dutch artist whose diverse practice spans sculpture, painting, ceramics, collage, video and textiles. His work addresses issues of autobiography, art history and societal violence and explores the tension between abstraction, expressionism and minimalism. He has exhibited nationally and internationally, most recently at Sogetsu Foundation, Tokyo (2023), Museum of Cycladic Art, Athens (2021), and Institute of Contemporary Art, Boston (2020). His work can be found in the collections of the Tate, London; Centre Pompidou, Paris; and Museum of Modern Art, New York, among others.

KATIE SCHWAB (b. 1985, London, UK)
Katie Schwab works with textiles, installation, sculpture and print. Her practice draws on historic textiles to reflect on moments of personal and social change. Developed through research in archives and community settings, her practice builds from craft practices, communal encounters and vibrant, abstract textile design to picture alternative futures for turbulent pasts. Recent exhibitions include *British Art Show 9*, Hayward Gallery Touring (2021–22), *small wares*, Vleeshal, the Netherlands (2021), and *Another Crossing: Artists Revisit the Mayflower Voyage*, Fuller Craft Museum, Massachusetts, USA (2020).

THOMSON (b. 1969, London, UK)
& CRAIGHEAD (b. 1971, Aberdeen, UK)
Jon Thomson and Alison Craighead have been working together since 1993. Using sound, video, installation and online space, Thomson & Craighead's recent work explores how globalisation and global communication networks are reshaping the way we perceive the world around us. They have exhibited widely in the UK and internationally and their work features in private and public collections, including the Imperial War Museum, Museum of London, Arts Council Collection, and the Victoria & Albert Museum.

BILL VIOLA (b. 1951, New York, USA; d. 2024)
Bill Viola was an American video and installation artist known for his explorations of the larger themes of life – birth, death, spirituality and existential introspection. He was instrumental in the establishment of video as a vital form of contemporary art and helped to greatly expand its scope in terms of technology, content and historical reach. His work has been exhibited widely and is held in a large number of public collections, including the Art Institute of Chicago; the Museum of Modern Art, New York; Tate, London; and Museum für Moderne Kunst, Frankfurt.

ALBERTA WHITTLE (b. 1980, Bridgetown, Barbados)
Alberta Whittle's multi-faceted practice is preoccupied with developing a personal response to the legacies of the Atlantic slave trade, unpicking its connections to institutional racism, white supremacy and climate emergency in the present. Against an oppressive political background, she aims to foreground hope and engage with different forms of resistance. Whittle represented Scotland at the 59th International Art Exhibition of La Biennale di Venezia (2022) and is a 2022 recipient of the Paul Hamlyn Awards for Artists. In 2020, she was awarded a Turner Bursary, the Frieze Artist Award, and a Henry Moore Foundation Artist Award. Whittle was the Margaret Tait Award winner for 2018/19. She lives and works in Glasgow, Scotland, received her PhD from Edinburgh College of Art in 2024, and is a current Research Associate at The University of Johannesburg.

RICHARD WILSON (b. 1953, London, UK)
Richard Wilson is one of Britain's most renowned sculptors. He makes sculptures, drawings, prints and sound performances and is internationally celebrated for his interventions in architectural space. Wilson has exhibited widely for over thirty-five years, with major museum exhibitions and public works in countries including Japan, China, the USA, Brazil, Mexico, Russia, Australia and Iraq, as well as throughout Europe. Wilson represented Britain in the Sydney, São Paulo and Venice Aperto biennials (1992, 1990 and 1986, respectively), and the Yokohama and Aichi Triennials (2005 and 2013). He has been nominated for the Turner Prize on two occasions (1988 and 1989) and was elected as a Royal Academician in 2006.

Zone
ENDS
SOUTH

AUTHOR BIOGRAPHIES

DR GUS CASELY-HAYFORD OBE
Dr Gus Casely-Hayford OBE is the inaugural Director of V&A East. He was previously Director of the Smithsonian National Museum of African Art and Executive Director of Arts Strategy of Arts Council England. He is a curator, cultural historian and broadcaster who writes, lectures, and has presented acclaimed BBC and Sky Arts series. He is a Fellow of King's College London and Jesus College, Cambridge, and was awarded an OBE in 2018 for his services to arts and culture.

EMMA DABIRI
Emma Dabiri is an academic, author and broadcaster who lived in East London for over twenty years. She is the author of *Disobedient Bodies, What White People Can Do Next* and *Don't Touch My Hair*. She has presented several television and radio programmes, including BBC Radio 4's *Journeys into Afro-Futurism*, BBC 2's *Back in Time for Brixton* and the Cannes Silver Lion award-winning *Hair Power* for Channel 4. She is a Fellow of the Royal Society of Literature and is in her final year of a PhD in Visual Sociology.

JES FERNIE
Jes Fernie is an independent curator, lecturer and writer. She works with galleries, visual arts organisations, universities and artists to make exhibitions, public artworks, residency projects and public programmes across the UK and abroad. Working primarily in the public realm, she is interested in how artworks are viewed, positioned and transformed by a live relationship with audiences, contexts and conditions. She is founder of the *Archive of Destruction* and lectures widely at institutions such as the Royal College of Art, Goldsmiths and Central Saint Martins.

ANDREW JONES
Andrew Jones writes about architecture, design, travel and cities. He has written for various publications, including the *Financial Times, Blueprint*, *The London Gardener* and *The World of Interiors*. He is the author of *The Buildings of Green Park*, a study of the built environment in Mayfair and St James's, and *The London Club*, both published by ACC Art Books. He is also a contributor to *Seeing Things*, which details 'the small wonders of the world according to writers, artists, and others.'

EDITOR BIOGRAPHIES

CHARLOTTE BOOTH
Charlotte Booth joined The Line in 2015 and is responsible for delivering the exhibition programme and the organisation's sustainability objectives. Her experience spans exhibitions, commissions and collections.

SARAH CARRINGTON
Sarah Carrington joined The Line in 2019 and was appointed Director in 2025. She has over twenty years of experience in shaping and delivering ambitious programmes in galleries and public spaces.

MEGAN PIPER
Megan Piper co-founded The Line with the late regeneration expert Clive Dutton OBE. She served as its Director from 2015 to 2025. Prior to setting up The Line, she was a gallerist in London's West End.

C.F. PRIOR
c.f. prior is a writer and editor. They are writing a book about the visual cultures of the end of life and are the founder of the writing collective *We Don't Write Alone*.

ACKNOWLEDGEMENTS

This book is dedicated to the memory of Clive Dutton OBE (1953–2015)

THE LINE WOULD LIKE TO THANK THE FOLLOWING

All the artists we have worked with over the years, whose remarkable contributions have enriched the waterways of East London and illuminated the pages of this book.

Our local residents, community partners, co-commissioners, schools and local organisations, whose insight and engagement have informed our programmes and helped to shape The Line.

The large number of landowners and stakeholders whose belief in The Line has made its existence possible and who continue to support its evolution. Special thanks to Beverley Charters at the House Mill and Simon Myers at Cody Dock, who have been part of our journey from the start. Their support and collaborative spirit have been at the heart of The Line's development.

The galleries and lenders, whose commitment and goodwill have enabled each installation on the route.

The crowdfunders who helped to initiate the project and our Founding Patrons and Supporters, without whom The Line wouldn't exist.

Our patrons and funders – past and present – for their faith and extraordinary generosity. Their commitment sustains us and makes everything you see in this book possible.

All the professionals – including fabricators, installers, lawyers, insurers, architects, engineers – that help to make the magic happen.

Collaborators – including Akademi, arebyte, Arup, English National Ballet, Foundation for Contemporary Art–Ghana, London Museum, London Youth Rowing, National Portrait Gallery, Royal Museums Greenwich – whose openness to working together has enriched and expanded the reach of our programme.

London College of Fashion, London College of Communication (UAL), UCL East, London Metropolitan University and University of East London – our academic partnerships have been instrumental in helping us to deepen our understanding of the impact of our work. Special thanks to Charlotte Hodes at London College of Fashion for her support of The Line through multiple programmes.

The team – everyone who has worked at The Line since its launch in 2015 – permanent staff as well as freelancers and Youth Guides – who have helped to create something extraordinary.

Our Trustees and Advisors – past and present – who give their time so generously and whose experience and expertise have contributed beyond measure, ensuring the good governance of the organisation and enabling it to thrive.

The curators we have been fortunate enough to collaborate with: Susie Allen, Laura Culpan, Sophie Dutton and Caroline Worthington.

Jennifer Greitschus at Arup Phase 2 with whom we have realised some of our most ambitious projects to date. Her creativity, vision and resourcefulness have led to a hugely rewarding collaboration.

The countless individuals who have contributed to our work in ways that would be impossible to attempt to capture here.

Everyone who has visited The Line and shared stories and photos, inspiring others through their own experiences.

MEGAN PIPER WOULD LIKE TO PERSONALLY THANK

The team, who have initiated programmes I couldn't have imagined and have grown the reach and impact of The Line through their energy, enthusiasm, and ideas.

Charlotte Booth and Sarah Carrington – the other two musketeers – whose commitment has made The Line's tenth anniversary possible. As a former colleague used to say, 'Teamwork makes the dream work'. And they prove it's true.

Owen and Sophie Dutton for their friendship and continuous support.

Tony Hales CBE, Ivan Harbour, Hanif Kara OBE, Matthew Moore, Lord Palumbo, Anne-Marie Piper, Nicola Stephenson, Richard Wadhams and Mark Wallinger, whose early belief in The Line was critical to its launch.

Friends and family who have held my hand; you know who you are. And finally, Jonathan and Jude for their love and patience.

IN RELATION TO THIS PUBLICATION

Christopher Jones and Philip Rebeiz for their dedication to making this book a reality. It would have been an unrealised dream without their generosity. Their continued commitment to our work underpins our success.

COLOUR THEMES

Keith Fox for his belief in the potential of this book and his early commitment to its realisation.

Carla Sakamoto, Senior Editor at Monacelli, for her guidance, expertise and encouragement throughout the publishing process.

Michael Vagnetti, whose eye for beautiful books has been key to the production process.

Tim Balaam and Kate Sclater of Hyperkit for their exceptional design, which truly brings the experience of The Line to life.

c.f. prior for the myriad ways they have contributed to this book, from copywriting to liaising with artists. They have helped to shape this publication from the outset and it has been a joy to work together.

Gus Casely-Hayford OBE for an illuminating conversation that shines a spotlight on The Line's journey, the context of the route and its relationship to the legacy of the Olympics.

The writers – Emma Dabiri, Jes Fernie and Andrew Jones – for their inspiring insights into The Line, the artworks, people and places that make it so special. They have captured the essence of the project so beautifully.

Those who generously gave their time to talk to Andrew Jones about their personal experience of The Line – Niyi Abidakun, Zenab Bhuta, Gino Brignoli, Helen Cammock, Beverley Charters, Mahtab Hussain, Nadia Kerbouche, Amar Lodhia, Simon Myers, Akif Rahman and Catherine Sizer – and Laura Hodgson for the exceptional portraits that accompany Andrew's essay.

Dr Ope Lori for her sensitivity read of the book.

Thierry Bal, Dan Marsh and Angus Mill for their unsurpassed photographic skill, advice and patience in capturing The Line on the ground and from the air. And all the photographers who have contributed to the book, whose brilliant work enhances these pages: Andrew Baker, Sim Canetty-Clarke, Andrea Capello, Stephen Chung, Diamond Geezer, Bill Green, Laura Hodgson, Ada Ihebom, Adam Kaleta, Emily Lovell, Jeff Moore, Nii Odzenma, Photography by ASH, Paul Popper/Popperfoto, Rebecca Reid, Vassilis Skopelitis, Andy Stagg, Reece Straw, Jim Stephenson, Chris Tubbs and Luis Veloso.

IMAGE CREDITS

Cover: Rasheed Araeen, *Discosailing* in Queen Elizabeth Olympic Park, 2024. Courtesy the artist and Grosvenor Gallery. Photograph: Stephen Chung/PinPep. © Rasheed Araeen. All Rights Reserved, DACS 2025
Back cover: Heron in Three Mills Wall River. Photograph: Angus Mill

T – top, B – bottom, C – centre, L – left, R – right

P.13 Photograph: Rebecca Reid
P.14 Photograph: Jim Stephenson
P.17 (L) Courtesy the artist and Pangolin London. Photograph: Diamond Geezer. (R) Courtesy private collection. Photograph: The Line © Damien Hirst and Science Ltd. All rights reserved, DACS 2025
P.18 Photograph: Paul Popper/Popperfoto via Getty Images
P.20 Photograph: © Ada Ihebom/Arup
P.24 Photograph: Thierry Bal
P.25 Photograph: The Line
P.29–35 All photographs: Laura Hodgson
P.37 Courtesy the artist and Simchowitz Gallery. Photograph: Thierry Bal
P.39 Film still: Adam Kaleta
P.41 Courtesy the artist and Bo Lee and Workman. Photograph: Dan Marsh
P.42 Film still: Helen Cammock. Courtesy the artist and Kate MacGarry, London
P.46 Youth Guides walking The Line with a member of the public at Greenwich Peninsula. Photograph: The Line
P.48 Courtesy the artist and Greenwich Peninsula. Photograph: Chris Tubbs
P.50 Courtesy the artists. Photograph: Angus Mill
P.52 Green Jetty at Greenwich Peninsula. Photograph: Angus Mill
P.54–55 Courtesy the artist. Photographs: Thierry Bal
P.56 Courtesy the artist. Photograph: Dan Marsh
P.57 Courtesy the artist. Photograph: Thierry Bal
P.58 Aerial view of The O2 and Canary Wharf, with Richard Wilson's *A Slice of Reality* and Serge Attukwei Clottey's *Tribe and Tribulation* visible on the river. Photograph: Dan Marsh
P.60 Courtesy the artist and Simchowitz Gallery. Photograph: Angus Mill
P.62 Courtesy the artist and Simchowitz Gallery, (T) Photograph: The Line. (B) Photograph: Thierry Bal
P.63 Courtesy the artist and Simchowitz Gallery. Photograph: Thierry Bal
P.64 Procession in London. All photographs: The Line
P.65 Processions in London and Accra. (T) Photograph: © Ada Ihebom/Arup / (B) & (3xR) Photographs: Nii Odzenma
P.66 Seal on the foreshore of the Thames at Greenwich Peninsula. Photograph: Bill Green
P.68–69 Courtesy the artist, Matthew Marks, and Sprüth Magers. Photographs: Thierry Bal. © Gary Hume. All Rights Reserved, DACS 2025
P.70 Gary Hume, *Liberty Grip* (2008) and Antony Gormley, *Quantum Cloud* (2000). Photograph: Dan Marsh
P.72 View across the Thames to Trinity Buoy Wharf. Photograph: Angus Mill
P.74 Courtesy the artist and Mayor of London. Photograph: Emily Lovell
P.76 Courtesy the artist and Mayor of London. Photograph: Angus Mill
P.78 Aerial view of City Hall and the Royal Docks from the London Cable Car. Photograph: Angus Mill
P.80 Courtesy the artist. Photograph: Luis Veloso
P.82 Courtesy the artist and Hauser & Wirth. Photograph: Luis Veloso. © Martin Creed. All Rights Reserved, DACS 2025
P.84 Courtesy the artist and Pangolin London. Photograph: Sim Canetty-Clarke. © The Paolozzi Foundation, Licensed by DACS 2025
P.85 Courtesy the artist and Pangolin London. Photograph: Diamond Geezer. © The Paolozzi Foundation, Licensed by DACS 2025
P.86 Courtesy the artist and Hannah Barry Gallery. Photograph: Andy Stagg
P.88 Reflection of the Royal Docks in the windows of City Hall. Photograph: Angus Mill
P.90 Courtesy the artist and Bo Lee and Workman. Photograph: Emily Lovell
P.91–93 Courtesy the artist and Bo Lee and Workman. Photographs: Thierry Bal
P.94–95 Courtesy London Borough of Newham Heritage Service. Photographs: Angus Mill
P.96 Courtesy the artist and Copperfield, London 2025. Photograph: Reece Straw. © Larry Achiampong. All rights reserved, DACS/Artimage
P.98 View of the London Cable Car over the Thames. Photograph: Angus Mill
P.100 View of the Royal Docks and Larry Achiampong, *What I Hear I Keep* (2022). Photograph: Reece Straw
P.102–103 Courtesy the artist and Royal Docks Team. Photographs: Angus Mill
P.104 View of City Hall, the Royal Docks and the London Cable Car. Photograph: Angus Mill
P.106 Courtesy London Borough of Newham Heritage Service. Photograph: Jeff Moore
P.108 Wildflowers on Cody Road. Photograph: Angus Mill
P.110–113 Courtesy the artist. All photographs: Thierry Bal
P.114 Entrance to Cody Dock. Photograph: Angus Mill
P.116 Courtesy private collection. Photograph: Sim Canetty-Clarke © Damien Hirst and Science Ltd. All rights reserved, DACS 2025
P.118 Courtesy the artist and l'étrangère. Photographs: The Line
P.120 Courtesy London Borough of Newham Heritage Service. Photograph: Angus Mill
P.122 Panoramic view across the River Lea to Tower Hamlets, including Madge Gill's *Nature in Mind* installation. Photograph: Angus Mill
P.124 Cody Dock Rolling Bridge, designed by Thomas Randall-Page, which launched in 2022. Photograph: Angus Mill
P.126–131 Courtesy the artist and Kate MacGarry, London. All photographs: Thierry Bal
P.132 View across the River Lea with Erno Goldfinger's Balfron Tower on the left and the dormer windows of Bromley Hall on the right. Photograph: Angus Mill
P.134 Courtesy the artist and Pangolin London. (L) Photograph: Vassilis Skopelitis (R) Photograph: Dan Marsh
P.136 Courtesy the artist and Pangolin London. Photograph: Thierry Bal
P.138 Courtesy the artist and Galerie Polaris. Photograph: Angus Mill. In memory of the stone engraver Daniel Griffin
P.139 Courtesy the artist and Galerie Polaris. Photograph: Dan Marsh
P.140–141 Courtesy the artist and Galerie Polaris. All photographs: Angus Mill
P.142 Runner on the River Lea. Photograph: Angus Mill
P.144 Courtesy the artist and Modern Art. Photograph: Thierry Bal
P.145 Courtesy the artist and Modern Art. Photograph: Andrea Capello
P.146 View of Bow Locks. Photograph: Angus Mill
P.148–149 Courtesy the artist and White Cube. Photographs: Angus Mill. © Tracey Emin. All rights reserved, DACS 2025
P.150 The House Mill and Clock Mill at Three Mills Island. Photograph: Angus Mill
P.152 Courtesy the artist and White Cube. Photograph: Angus Mill
P.153 Courtesy the artist and White Cube. Photograph: Thierry Bal
P.154 Aerial view looking south towards The O2 and Canary Wharf, with Bow Locks and Bromley-by-Bow Gasworks in the middle distance. Photograph: Dan Marsh
P.156 The House Mill at Three Mills Island. Photograph: Laura Hodgson
P.158–159 Courtesy the artist and Southern & Partners. Photographs: Kira Perov © Bill Viola
P.160 Installation view of Alberta Whittle, *between a whisper and a cry*, 2019. Courtesy the artist and The Modern Institute/Toby Webster Ltd, Glasgow. Photograph: The Line. © Alberta Whittle. All rights reserved, DACS 2025
P.162 Film still: Martha Atienza. Courtesy the artist and Silverlens
P.163 Film still: Ursula Biemann. Courtesy the artist
P.164 Installation view of Ursula Biemann, *Deep Weather* (2013). Courtesy the artist. Photograph: The Line
P.166 Film still: Martin Edelsteen. Courtesy Hanna Ljungh and Filmform
P.167 Film still: Daniela Medina Poch & Elizabeth Gallón Droste. Courtesy the artists
P.168 Film still: Alberta Whittle. Courtesy the artist and The Modern Institute/Toby Webster Ltd, Glasgow. © Alberta Whittle. All rights reserved, DACS 2025
P.169 Film still: Helen Cammock. Courtesy the artist and Kate MacGarry, London
P.170 Heron and little egret in the Channelsea River by Three Mills. Photograph: Angus Mill
P.172 Courtesy London Borough of Newham Heritage Service. Photograph: Angus Mill
P174. Grey mullet in the Channelsea River by Three Mills. Photograph: Angus Mill
P.176–177 Courtesy private collection. Photographs: Vassilis Skopelitis © Thomas J Price
P.178 *Reaching Out* and Cllr Charlene McLean. Courtesy the artist and Hauser & Wirth. Photograph: Andrew Baker © Thomas J Price
P.179 Courtesy the artist and Hauser & Wirth. Photograph: Vassilis Skopelitis © Thomas J Price

P.180 View north on Three Mills Wall River, including Phaidon's London office. Photograph: Angus Mill
P.182 Courtesy the artist. Photograph: Angus Mill. In memory of Valli van Zijl
P.184–185 Courtesy the artist. Photographs: Reece Straw
P.186 Aerial view of Somang Lee's *The Living Line*, looking towards Queen Elizabeth Olympic Park. Photograph: Dan Marsh
P.188–189 Courtesy London Borough of Newham Heritage Service. Photographs: Angus Mill
P.190 Aerial view of East Bank and London Aquatics Centre. Photograph: Dan Marsh
P.192 Courtesy the artist and Grosvenor Gallery. Photograph: Dan Marsh. © Rasheed Araeen. All Rights Reserved, DACS 2025
P.193 Courtesy the artist and Grosvenor Gallery. Photograph: Stephen Chung/PinPep. © Rasheed Araeen. All Rights Reserved, DACS 2025
P.194 Courtesy the artist and Grosvenor Gallery. Photograph: Dan Marsh. © Rasheed Araeen. All Rights Reserved, DACS 2025
P.195 Courtesy the artist and Grosvenor Gallery. Photograph: Stephen Chung/PinPep. © Rasheed Araeen. All Rights Reserved, DACS 2025
P.196 Courtesy the artist. Photograph: Angus Mill. © Anish Kapoor. All rights reserved, DACS 2025
P.198 Courtesy the artist and Gagosian. Photograph: Emily Lovell. © DACS 2025
P.200 View of UCL (University College London) East, Anish Kapoor's *ArcelorMittal Orbit* and Carsten Höller's *The Slide* in Queen Elizabeth Olympic Park. Photograph: Angus Mill. © Anish Kapoor. All Rights Reserved, DACS 2025
P.202–205 Courtesy the artist. All photographs: Reece Straw
P.206 View of V&A East; London College of Fashion, UAL; BBC Music Studios; and Sadler's Wells East in Queen Elizabeth Olympic Park. Photograph: Angus Mill
P.208 Detail: Anne Hardy, *Destination London* (2021). Courtesy the artist and Maureen Paley
P.210 Courtesy the artists. Photograph: Vassilis Skopelitis
P.212 Courtesy the artist and Maureen Paley. Photograph: Angus Mill
P.214 Courtesy the artist and Kate MacGarry, London. Photograph: Angus Mill
P.216 Collaboration with English National Ballet and ROKSANDA at the launch of Rana Begum's *No. 1104 Catching Colour*. Photographs: Photography by ASH
P.220 (T) Photograph: Angus Mill. (B) Courtesy the artist. Photograph: Reece Straw
P.223 Photograph: Angus Mill
P.225 Photograph: Angus Mill
P.233 The Line's signage near Star Lane station. Photograph: The Line
P.238: Procession at Greenwich Peninsula led by Serge Attukwei Clottey and One-Drum Foundation. Photograph: The Line

Monacelli
A Phaidon Company
111 Broadway
New York, NY 10006

Phaidon Press Limited
2 Cooperage Yard
London E15 2QR

Phaidon SARL
55, rue Traversière
75012 Paris

phaidon.com/monacelli

First published 2025

ISBN 978-1-58093-695-8

Library of Congress Control Number: 2025904977

Editor: Carla Sakamoto
Production: Michael Vagnetti
Design: Hyperkit
Printed in China